This book is dedicated to you—

*The one who knows where you are isn't where you want to
be and refuses to settle for the status quo.*

*Comfort is attractive. It's easy to stay there.
But you feel pulled toward a big goal for a reason.
I applaud you for stepping into the unknown
and for choosing the more challenging path
toward a life of purpose and growth.*

You're exactly where change begins. Keep going.

I HOPE
I MAKE YOU
UNCOMFORTABLE

Start Before You're Ready.
Grow Beyond What You Imagined.

RASHELLE MASON

I Hope I Make You Uncomfortable
Start Before You're Ready. Grow Beyond What You Imagined.

Paperback ISBN: 978-1-967587-93-3
eBook ISBN: 978-1-967587-94-0
Hardcover ISBN: 978-1-967587-95-7

Design and cover art by Peaceful Profits.

CONTENTS

Introduction:
"YOU ARE FINE"

Three hours into my attempt at breaking the world record for the longest female elbow plank, my left arm went numb.

I'd been training for almost a year, and numbness was nothing new. When you plank for hours at a time, your limbs start to feel puffy—like when you hike in humid weather and your fingers swell. Then, an arm, leg, or foot might fall asleep. But usually, I could pump my fist, shift my weight, or wiggle my toes and regain sensation.

Not today.

As thousands of people cheered me on from every corner of the gymnasium, I rocked back and forth on my mat. Nothing. Whatever nerve I'd pinched, it wasn't letting go. And with the Guinness World Record officials watching, I couldn't break form, not even to move my arm through its range of motion. I wasn't allowed to pick my limbs up at all. The numbness grew worse, and I felt my arm trying to collapse.

The record I needed to beat was four hours, thirty minutes, and eleven seconds.

I was aiming for five hours.

As I pushed toward the last hour, my core and three limbs kept me in the plank position. Because I was working harder than usual, I was sweating more than I did during training. Water cascaded off me like a running faucet, and my arms slid on the mat.

I could feel a shift in the room, like stagnant energy had filled the air. I could almost hear the crowd thinking, *Uh-oh… she's struggling.*

"Fifty-nine minutes left!" My husband, Shan, shouted.

I winced and tried to tune everything out. My focus narrowed to the mantra I'd written in black ink on the inside of my forearm:

"YOU ARE FINE!"

That's what I told myself during training.

You are fine. This is temporary. You're not going to die.

I had written that because our minds jump straight to the worst-case scenario when we push ourselves beyond our comfort zone. The worst-case scenario in life is death, and I knew this wasn't that. I was okay. I just had to keep going.

I looked up in search of another distraction from the pain. I saw the American flag on the platform in front of me, the red, white, and blue balloons overhead, and people in the crowd planking in solidarity. The digital countdown clock flashed white numbers as time ticked on. Whistles and shouts grew louder, punctuated with encouragement.

"Come on!"

"You've got it!"

"Let's go, Rashelle!"

And in came Shan's familiar voice again, "Fifty-eight minutes!"

Oh no.

"Honey, I can't hear that right now," I said.

Then my brain proposed the distraction I didn't know I needed.

I looked up at my husband and said, "Go get Andy."

Our neighbor Andy was the reason we turned my world record day into a fundraiser for the *Catch A Lift Fund,* a nonprofit that helps combat-injured veterans recover and find purpose through fitness. I hadn't planned to get him involved in that final hour, but I was starting to get scared that I wouldn't make it to the end. Something in me knew I didn't need encouragement—I needed perspective.

I needed something to minimize what I was going through, because I *would* be fine when this was over. Andy *wasn't* fine after his military experience. I didn't know his full story, but I knew what he had endured would make fifty-eight more minutes of planking seem like nothing.

Andy looked surprised when he walked up to my platform. "What do you need?"

"I need your help," I said.

"You've got it—whatever I can do. Want me to make you laugh?"

"No!" I said quickly. No telling what laughing would do to my stability.

"I need you to tell me what happened in Iraq."

He paused. "You want the whole story?"

"I've got time!"

So, Andy pulled up a chair and started talking.

He told me about his two tours serving as a sniper in Iraq, the friends he watched die, the lives he had to take, and the trauma he brought home. He talked about the years he numbed the pain with drugs and alcohol and his fight to get clean.

Andy's story did what I'd hoped it would. He helped me burn twenty minutes off the clock, and he made what I was doing feel much smaller—silly, even. That was exactly what I needed to get through it. I thought, *If he can come home from war, overcome addiction, and stay clean for six years and counting, all while still dealing with dark days and triggers, this planking thing really is nothing.*

I can do this, I thought. But my arm was still numb, so that's when I decided to shift my focus. I wasn't trying to hit five hours anymore. I just wanted to stay planking past the record time. I wanted to see the confetti fly.

After that, time moved faster. I thought about the version of me who'd wake up tomorrow morning. I wanted her to be proud. She wouldn't care as much about how long I lasted. She just needed to know that I'd done everything I possibly could to achieve this goal, and totally emptied my tank. As long as that was true, I'd be okay with myself tomorrow. I just couldn't fail knowing I had something left to give.

My son, Kole, shouted, "Nine minutes left!"

By then, I welcomed the countdown. With Andy's help, I'd gotten my mind to a place where I could handle it, but it was still a brutal fight to the end. I've had three kids, run two marathons, and I can tell you with confidence that I've never fought harder in my life than I did that day.

Approaching the record time, people started crying, grabbing each other's hands, and yelling as loudly as they could. Every time I shifted on the mat, they grimaced, like they were gunning for the world record, too. The cheers got louder, and my body screamed along with the crowd, until finally…

"Five!"

"Four!"

"Three!"

"Two!"

"One!"

I did it. I made it past the record time. Then, nine seconds later, my body gave out.

I fell into child's pose, and my arms couldn't even lift me upright to face the crowd. But from the moment I collapsed, I felt exactly how I thought I would. I was the most depleted I'd ever been, my arms still numb, and my elbows raw and bleeding. But the mental struggle was gone.

From there, it was up to Guinness to review the attempt and determine if it was official. But in that moment, I honestly didn't care. With my people cheering around me and the hardest year of training under my belt, I felt like I'd already won. I was hit with instant clarity that this was about more than a record; it was about community, unimaginable growth, and finding out what I was capable of.

Face-down on that sweat-soaked mat, I was smiling. *I was fine.*

The Hardest Part of Any Challenge

People think the hardest part of a challenge like this is the physical side. It's not.

Sure, my body was working hard. But the real fight was in my head. That's where I had to wrestle with the doubt, fear, and discomfort that tempted me to give up before my tank was empty. Without a reserve of tools I knew supported me, and *proof* that I could do this, I may not have made it to the end that day.

Your body will do whatever your mind tells it to. Planking for more than four hours with a numb arm confirmed that for me.

The most important skill to build? Mental toughness.

And by that, I don't mean burying your feelings or pretending the hard thing isn't hard. I mean the mental toughness you need to show up and stay present with discomfort, so you can achieve your goals *anyway*.

Mental toughness is built in discomfort. You can't make your biggest, scariest dreams happen without it, whether it's a physical challenge, a professional goal, or anything else you hope to achieve. So, discomfort is a good thing. Feeling uncomfortable is a necessary part of doing anything worthwhile.

Here's Why This Book Exists

This book isn't about me breaking a world record. It's about *your* audacious goal.

Maybe the goal in your mind is pursuing a physical feat, going after a job that feels too ambitious, or something completely different. Perhaps you've worked toward something daunting before, but you kept hitting a wall. Or maybe you're just tired of letting discomfort hold you back in general.

I wrote this book because I've been there.

At 53, I decided to attempt to break a world record, but I'm not sure 23-year-old Rashelle could have pulled off everything that goal required. I wasn't always the person who could fight her way through something that hard, despite the numbness and pain.

I didn't have the mental toughness to get through something like this back then. But I've spent years building it through failures, small wins, major setbacks, and plenty of uncomfortable moments that didn't end with balloons and confetti.

This book shares the skills, tools, and steps that made my mind tough enough to achieve anything I decide to, and shows you how to build the same strength. Because discomfort shouldn't stop you from reaching your potential. You just need the mental toughness to move forward anyway.

If you're stuck, overwhelmed, or craving more but aren't sure how to get there, this book is for you. In the pages that follow, you'll learn how to:

- start before you feel ready,
- reframe failure as feedback,
- stay present through discomfort,
- keep going when motivation disappears,
- follow through on what you said you'd do, and
- walk away proud, no matter the outcome.

You don't need a perfect plan. Show up on day one. Then the day after that. Repeat until your "world record day" arrives. This book will help you do that.

How I've Laid It Out

To make this book as useful as possible, I've structured it to help you take action, not just get inspired. Here's how it's mapped out:

- **Part 1: Mindset Reset**—clarify your "why," push past roadblocks, and get in the right headspace to start and stick with the journey toward your goal
- **Part 2: Rise and Begin**—how to build momentum toward your goal, set achievable milestones, and keep going even when you feel like quitting

- **Part 3: The Big Day and Beyond**–what happens when you reach your goal and how to move forward without losing yourself in the aftermath

Each chapter starts with an intention, just like you would at the beginning of a yoga practice, to set the tone and focus your energy on the steps in front of you.

This isn't a book to read passively. It's designed to help you build your personal toolkit, so you can go from overwhelmed and stuck to pursuing all of the big, hard things you want for yourself.

Along the way, you'll also find a few invitations to work with me through personalized wellness coaching if that feels like a supportive next step. You know your needs best, but my services are available to explore anytime they might help you reach a goal.

Final Note: I Hope This Book Makes You Uncomfortable

This book won't make you the toughest person in the room. It won't prevent you from having hard days. And it won't enable you to achieve things without needing support.

But it *will* push you to face your fears. It *will* ask you to fight through discomfort. It *will* help you find the right support so you can fight harder than you ever have and wake up proud that you fully emptied your tank.

That might sound exciting now, but eventually you'll want to quit. A day will come when quitting sounds like the best idea you've ever had. That's when you pick up this book and remind yourself not to avoid discomfort, but to *hope* for it.

Because on the other side of discomfort is the version of you who achieved the goal in your mind today. That version of you can wake up the next morning and look in the mirror, totally depleted, with battle scars and a smile, and say: *I'm fine.*

To getting uncomfortable,

Rashelle Mason

P.S. Want to see what those final moments looked like? Watch the seven-minute video of my world record plank attempt at https://youtu.be/s9O72v-sbL8.

PART 1

MINDSET RESET

Chapter 1
WHY FIRST

Don't be consistent to impress others.
Don't practice discipline for praise.
What keeps you going when no one claps—
when you're tired, alone, and scared?
That's your "why."
Find it and show up for it daily.

—

I didn't start my planking journey because I wanted to break a world record. It started with a fitness challenge that popped up in my Facebook feed in the spring of 2024.

The goal was to plank daily, increasing your time by one minute each day. I thought, *Hey, why not?* It sounded like a fun way to push myself a little, and that was reason enough to start. I'd roll out a yoga mat, watch the timer on my phone, feel the burn, and then move on with my day.

I kept adding time to my plank, and when I hit sixteen minutes, I was officially impressed with myself. *I wonder how long I can actually hold this?*

But things didn't get serious until I lost my job.

Before July 4, 2024, I was the vice president of sales at a company I loved. I led people, coached teams, managed a multi-million-dollar budget, and took a lot of pride in my work. I wasn't fired; the company just went out of business. But it still felt like failure.

At first, I tried to stay positive. I thought, *I should find a similar role pretty quickly. I have a good track record, so why wouldn't I get hired?* Then weeks went by. I applied to hundreds of jobs, received countless rejections, and started to feel embarrassed about my situation.

But all the while, I kept up my silly little planking thing.

Planking became something that helped me feel capable, a way to prove to myself that I could endure hard things. Even if a dozen rejections came through that day, I could still hit the mat and fight my way to a new personal best. So I could get through this, too.

One day, I was chatting with my next-door neighbor who works for Amazon. He mentioned they were short on delivery drivers with the holidays coming up, and I started asking questions.

"What's the pay like? How long are the shifts? Do drivers get benefits?"

It wasn't anything like the other jobs I was applying for. But the more I learned, the more I started to think this could be good for me. A steady routine. Something to get me out of the house. A way to stop spiraling and start moving again.

Interesting.

Around that time, my phone must have heard me talking about my planking challenge, because I opened Facebook and saw a story about DonnaJean Wilde, a Canadian woman in her fifties who broke the Guinness World Record for the longest female plank a few months earlier. Four hours, thirty minutes, and eleven seconds.

Interesting.

Delivering Amazon packages and attempting to break a world record aren't pursuits that would typically pique my interest. These two opportunities could have been random bits of information I disregarded as irrelevant, and they may seem completely unrelated. But they had landed in my world at the perfect time. Somehow, they both felt like the right kind of challenge to propel me forward.

I needed things to put my full focus into, so I could stop beating myself up about the job loss. I knew I could drive, and I knew I could plank for what (to me) was an impressive amount of time. Both of these ideas might have sounded crazy to me earlier that year, but suddenly, I found myself wondering:

Could I deliver packages?

Could I break a world record?

So instead of letting the lack of purpose I felt chip away at my confidence, I grabbed at the opportunities that appeared in front of me. I applied for both.

I didn't mean for it to unfold this way, but these two decisions marked a turning point for me. Rather than allowing shame and embarrassment to consume me during a dark season of life, I let two unlikely pursuits give my days meaning. I stopped waiting for my life to go back to normal and started building something new.

Putting on my Amazon vest, loading up the van, and carrying packages through the freezing Wisconsin winter showed me I could contribute in meaningful ways I hadn't even considered. That feeling of moving forward anyway, and thriving despite the circumstances, became something I craved.

Then, my application to break the planking world record was accepted, and suddenly, this wasn't just a fitness challenge anymore. I had a training regimen to map out.

Most days, setting out to break a world record felt crazy, lonely, painful, and hard. But it also strengthened my mindset and showed me what I was capable of at a time when I needed the reminder.

If I hadn't lost my job, I don't think I would've attempted to break the world record—or even applied in the first place. That low point forced me to reckon with feelings of self-doubt and find stuff to cling to, even in unexpected places. Giving myself purpose didn't just sound nice; it was necessary to get me through that season. This became the deeper "why" behind the biggest goal I'd ever set in my life.

You need a "why" behind yours, too.

It's easy to chase goals when things are going well. But if you have a big, scary goal in mind right now, you have some of your toughest days ahead of you. The reward is worth the struggle, but you won't last long enough to see it if you don't have a "why" to push you forward. So let's start there.

What Makes a Powerful "Why"

When most people set a goal, they jump to what they want or how they'll do it.

I want to break this record. Here's the training I'll follow.

But when word got out about my planking goal, guess what people asked me first?

Not what, not how, but *why*.

If you have a big goal, your community will ask why you're pursuing it. It makes sense that they'll be curious. But here's something you may not anticipate: The person who asks you why you're doing this more than anyone else will be you.

When it's 4:00 a.m., and your alarm goes off to train at the gym.

When you have a stack of rejection letters on your desk.

When you walk up to speak in front of a crowd, and need to overcome stage fright.

Your mind will ask, *Why?! Why am I doing this?*

It will tempt you to snooze your alarm, quit trying, or run away and hide. It wants you to be comfortable because, to your brain, comfort means you're safe. So you need a "why" that's powerful enough to quiet that voice. You need a reason that makes the discomfort worth it. Here are the two criteria that make a powerful "why."

Criteria Number 1: It has to mean something to you.

If you don't care deeply about the outcome you're aiming for, you're setting yourself up to fail. For example, I'd like to know more about investing, but I don't care enough to work on that. I could buy all of the books in the world about the stock market, but I already know I wouldn't have a clear "why" to keep going when it got confusing or dull.

Say you decide to run a marathon, but your main "why" is to post a medal selfie on Instagram or have something to talk about at your high school reunion. That won't carry you through mile fifteen on a freezing, rainy morning when your legs feel like lead, you've lost a toenail, and every step hurts.

If you enter a pie baking contest to impress your mom, but you don't even *like* pie, you won't spend weekends in the kitchen testing recipes. Eventually, you'll skip the practice bakes to hang out with friends—because it's not really your dream.

Your "why" has to matter to *you*, not your parents, your partner, or your social media followers.

If you're not sure what you care about, look at what makes you jealous of others. Jealousy gets a bad reputation, but it can be useful. It shines a light on what you value. I wouldn't care if someone beat me in a pie baking contest, but I'd be jealous if they beat me in a race. That says something about what matters to me.

When you're working toward something you care about, you'll keep showing up because you *want* to.

Criteria Number 2: It has to be deeper than the activity itself.

Even if your goal matters to you, you have to dig deeper than the thing itself. You don't run a marathon just because you're a decent runner. You don't get better with money because reading about the stock market is fun. You don't win a pie baking contest because you're passionate about good dessert.

Surface-level motivation can get you started, but *meaning* is what keeps you consistent and disciplined in the fight toward your goal.

It has to become more than a habit. When my alarm went off at 4:00 a.m. for training, I wouldn't have leapt out of bed, layered up in the dark, scraped frost off the windshield, and driven to the gym to plank in silence—just me, my thoughts, and my burning muscles—for bragging rights. Without a deeper reason, I would've hit snooze, curled back under the warm comforter, and said, "Ten more minutes."

Instead, I got up almost excited about training. It was painful and uncomfortable, but the fear and doubt became: *I know what this is going to give me.* The discomfort didn't feel like an obstacle because I knew exactly why I was doing it and what I was getting out of the process.

After I lost my job, I started to *need* the reward that came with completing something hard. The "why" behind my planking challenge became "to give myself purpose." It kept my hope alive. I thought, *If I can do this, I can find another job, too. There are so many things I can do—so many things I will do.*

Your biggest goals, the ones most worthy of pursuit, will push you face-first into the mud, again and again. They'll give you your most epic wins *and* your most brutal wipe-outs. So dig as deep as you can get right now. Peel back layers of the onion until you reach the deepest "why" you can find. Let's talk about how to do that.

How to Find Your "Why"

What I don't want is for you to procrastinate working toward your goal because you need the perfect "why" first. So, let's agree on something right now. We're going to walk through a few steps to find your deepest "why." Then, no matter what you uncover, you're going to get moving toward your goal. Deal?

The best way to find your "why" is simply to ask yourself… *Why?*

Why do I want this?
Why does it *need* to happen?
Why does that matter to me?
Why would I keep going on hard days?
Why would the reward be worth the discomfort?
Why would I pursue this goal, even if no one knew?

You may start with a superficial goal and arrive at something much deeper. It may not happen all at once, but see how far you can get by asking yourself "why." Here's what this process would have looked like for my planking journey:

Why are you planking?

Because I'm doing a fitness challenge. It's good for me.

But why do you need to plank for sixteen minutes?

Because it feels good to do hard things.

Okay, why keep going? Most people don't plank for twenty minutes.

Because now I'm curious. I want to see what my body can do.

Great, but why pursue the world record?

Because I lost my job, and this training makes me feel strong and confident. The reward feels better than punishing myself for my circumstances.

Why not do something else to get that reward? Something easier?

Because this is harder than anything I've ever done, but unlike my job search, it's something I can control. It gives me purpose and shows me that I'm still capable of extraordinary things.

Keep digging until your answer feels sturdy enough to stand up against the voice in your head that will want to hit "snooze" instead of training at 4:00 a.m. Your "why" should be the thing that makes this goal feel like something you *need* to do, not just something nice to have.

You Don't Need the Full Picture Yet

When I started planking, I didn't know I'd attempt to break a record *or* write a book. I didn't even have a great answer when people asked why I joined that initial Facebook challenge. It sounded like a fun way to push myself, but it grew into so much more.

Losing my job, something I never could've predicted, caused my "why" to shift. The training went from a lighthearted challenge to something I needed to keep me going. But because I'd already chosen to start, I was ready to attach deeper meaning to this goal when life demanded more from me.

That's how this works a lot of the time. If you don't have the most profound reason for pursuing your goal yet, that's okay. If you want to run a marathon, you won't know how those endorphins feel in your body until you start training. If you want to write a book, you won't find clarity until you get a few messy chapters written out.

Your "why" will evolve as you do. What starts as curiosity may end up giving you purpose, just like it did for me. With the big, daring goals we're talking about here, it's impossible to know everything you'll get out of the journey until you take the first step.

So don't skip this, but don't overthink it either.

Just find something that matters enough to get you started. If it gets you to show up on day one, trust it. As the days get harder, revisit your "why." Ask yourself what's helping you keep going even when you're uncomfortable. Ask what gets you up in the morning thinking, *Training day! Let's go!,* instead of staying in your warm bed. Eventually, you'll land on the "why" that gets you over the finish line.

At first, you'll have to push yourself to follow through. There will be days when your mind throws a dozen excuses at you, and you'll have to show up anyway. But if this goal really matters to you, you'll get to a point where you don't avoid the work to get there anymore. You'll look forward to it. I started catching myself thinking, *What time is it? I want to get going. I want to go train.* Something that once felt impossible became something I looked forward to, because I knew the powerful reward it was giving me mentally, emotionally, and spiritually.

When you feel that, you know your "why" is working. Keep showing up, and you'll find it.

Showing Up Is Enough

In the fitness classes I teach at the Princeton Club, I always finish by saying:

"Take a moment to thank yourself for coming."

As your heart rate comes down after taking one step toward a bigger goal, it's tempting to jump ahead to the next task on your list. But this is a valuable moment for reflection.

If you journal, you can write down how you feel. But this isn't a homework assignment. It's more like an invitation to notice what happens inside when you show up despite the odds. Even if it wasn't your best day—your run was slow, your writing was clunky, or you burned the pie—you showed up.

Hold space for whatever bubbles to the surface. You might find clues about why you're really in this. You could find the first glimmers of a bigger dream than you anticipated when you started, all because you put in work toward your goal today.

If all of my plans in life had gone exactly as I wanted, I'd still be in my position as the vice president of sales. I never would've pushed myself to find purpose in unlikely places, like in the driver's seat of an Amazon delivery van or on the floor holding the plank position for hours at a time. Because I kept showing up, even on the tough days, I found the strength to believe I could break that world record—the hardest thing I've ever attempted to do.

So thank yourself for showing up today. Reading this book means you're already on a path that could lead somewhere extraordinary that you can't even envision yet. As long as you've determined a "why" that will push you to show up tomorrow, you're in good shape.

That's how it starts.

Now, *just start.*

Get personalized support to move toward your goal.

If you want one-on-one coaching to define your big goal and stay accountable throughout the journey, I'm here to help. Start with a free thirty-minute consultation, and together we'll create a custom plan that fits your life and keeps you moving forward.

Visit www.riseshineco.com for coaching and speaking inquiries.

Chapter 2

JUST START

Claim what you want from life.
Have the courage to ask for it out loud.
Ask before you're ready.
Before you believe it's possible.
Your wildest dreams can seek you, too.
But only if you ask them to.

—

Someone asked me recently if I felt "ready" when my world record application was accepted. I laughed and replied, "Um…No!"

The truth is, I gave myself an out at every stage.

When I applied, I didn't know if I'd be accepted. Guinness gets over one thousand applications each week, and they can turn away anyone who doesn't meet certain criteria. The record for longest female plank was broken the same year I submitted my application, so I figured that might be reason enough to deny me. As my cursor hovered over the "Apply" button, I thought:

They probably won't accept you anyway. Applying doesn't cost anything. No one knows you're doing this. Just apply. It doesn't mean you have to do it.

Click. I applied. On the confirmation page, I saw a note that I'd have to wait up to twelve weeks to hear back. Below that, there was a big, red button that said "Cancel Application." I kept training through that waiting period, but every now and then, I thought, *You still have an out! All you have to do is click that red button anytime, and this whole thing goes away.*

Then I found out I had been accepted.

Was I excited? Yes. Was I nervous? YES. Was I *ready?* No.

As I read the acceptance notification, that red "Cancel" button glared back at me. It was still front and center on my Guinness dashboard, tempting me with a retreat back to comfort. I'd resisted clicking it before, but it looked even more enticing now.

The red button represented all of the "outs" I'd tried to give myself up to that point—a permission slip to stay on the fence instead of fully going for this goal. Really, that was my mind trying to wrestle back control over something that felt unfamiliar and *uncomfortable.* If I stayed uncertain, I didn't have to admit how unprepared I felt. If I pressed that red button, I couldn't fail.

Luckily, something in me knew better than to click "Cancel Application." I had already chosen a goal I cared about. I already had a "why" that had propelled me to show up for training so far. I realized this internal conflict wasn't about waiting to feel ready. On a subconscious level, I was just waiting to stop feeling uncomfortable.

The thing is, you'll never be ready to work toward a big goal. If you feel ready to accomplish all of your wildest dreams today, you aren't dreaming big enough. Readiness is a myth. It's your brain's way of keeping you on the "safe" path instead of the unfamiliar one. Because to your brain, unfamiliar means "potentially dangerous." But for the greatest things you'll do in this life, you'll have to bring fear, doubt, and discomfort along for the ride.

So, let's talk about how to do that. How do you move forward before you believe in yourself? How do you take the first step without knowing how you'll get to the finish line? You don't need all of the answers now. You just need to decide one thing:

Does your goal matter enough to begin?

The Courage to Begin Anyway

On the outside, it might look like people who do brave, bold things aren't afraid. Like they have a level of confidence you're lacking. That's not true. They just started anyway. But how do you get your mind to a place where you can "just start" before you feel ready?

If you want to run a marathon, you may think to yourself, *I don't know if I can do this.* But if you don't have any physical limitations preventing you from training, that thought isn't about your body. It's about your mind.

Running a marathon sounds scary if you've never done it before. Your brain doesn't yet know what this will require. It doesn't know how painful training might be, or how much time it'll take. So the excuses that come up aren't reasons to back down. They're just your mind's way of saying, *I don't have enough information to predict the outcome here. Without that intel, the best conclusion I can draw is that we should stay safe instead.*

When you realize your brain defaults to the safest option, you can stop mistaking that instinct for a sign that you shouldn't pursue your goals. This discomfort isn't a reason to stop. It means you're stepping into growth. You need the courage to override these thoughts and show up for what you want, even when you don't yet have the intel your brain is requesting.

And you've already taken a step in that direction. You set a *big* goal, despite how daunting, uncomfortable, or even impossible it may feel to picture yourself achieving it. Trust that we'll get to the logistics. We'll break down your timeline and the bite-sized, daily steps from your current reality to life *after* achieving this goal in Parts 2 and 3 of this book. That way, you know exactly how to work backward to get there. And most importantly, your mind can't use *not knowing* as an excuse anymore.

For now, let's focus on what you *do* know. If your goal is a marathon, and you can only run two miles today, great. There was a time when every marathoner could only run two miles. So, there *is* a path from here to there, even if it's not clear yet. Just hold onto the belief that you can start with two miles and eventually build up to 26.2.

That's what I did when I started training for the plank record. I didn't know what I was doing. You can't search "how to plank for five hours" and find a proven training plan. I didn't know what gear I'd need or how I'd stay motivated. But I didn't let that stop me. I kept showing up and pieced things together as I went.

If you've ever done something scary like skydiving or even riding a roller coaster, you've activated the courage I'm talking about here. As you gear up for the big moment, you oscillate between feeling excited and terrified. Your palms sweat and your brain yells, *Don't do it!* But then you do it, and the second it's over, you think, *I'm so glad I did that.*

If you've ever wanted to do something scary and backed out, you know that the regret of *not* doing it is always worse than the thing itself. Even giving something your all and failing is better than wondering what would've happened if you'd just started. Regret lingers, weighs you down, and leads to more self-doubt in the future.

On the other hand, doing the scary thing, like jumping out of that airplane, is over quickly. Through action, the fear gets alchemized into something better. You get to keep that memory in your "bag of proof," along with other past successes, as a reminder that you can pull it out anytime you doubt yourself. So when the next challenge comes, you can say, "I've done scary things before. I can do this one, too."

You may not see yourself as someone who was built to work toward big goals, so here's some proof you can add to your bag now. At one point, you were a baby who didn't know how to walk. You didn't worry about having the perfect plan to go from rolling over to crawling to walking. You didn't even realize you couldn't walk. It was just something you wanted to do, so you started trying.

How many times did you fall when you were learning to walk? Too many to count. But babies don't see falling as failure. They don't feel ashamed. They don't look around to see how many times other babies have fallen. They often laugh, get back up, and keep trying.

You were born with the courage to begin before you're ready. You can channel that now. Expect to fall. Expect to feel clumsy and awkward. That's not a sign you're doing this wrong. It's part of pursuing any challenge.

Starting anyway means being willing to be "bad" at something before you're good. Every time a baby falls, they learn something new about what it takes to stay standing. You have to be willing to take imperfect action, pay attention to what doesn't work, and use those lessons to optimize the path as you go.

Eventually, you'll stop fearing the fall and start celebrating it. Because now you get to ask yourself, *Why didn't that work? What can I do differently next time?* That's when you grow the most.

Your Official Commitment: Say It Out Loud

I didn't stop giving myself "outs" about the planking world record until I told the CEO of the Princeton Club where I train and teach fitness classes. I had to let him know I wanted to use the gym as the location for my world record attempt. That's when it finally felt like a real commitment to me. I'd said it out loud, so now it was really happening.

This is where I go against a lot of advice you've probably heard.

You always hear people say things like, "Keep your goals to yourself. Put your head down. Don't talk about it; just do the work." And I agree that working toward your goals should mean less talking, more action. But keeping goals to myself doesn't work for me.

I always say them out loud, for three reasons:

1. If I say it, that means I'm doing it.

This is about keeping promises to myself and the people I care about. It doesn't matter if it's running a marathon or planning a trip with a friend, I don't say things that I don't intend to follow through on.

Plus, every time I do something I say I'm going to do, I get to add it to my "bag of proof" that I am the person I claim to be. In the process, I become more and more familiar with how good it feels to follow through on my goals, even when they're scary. The more deposits I make into that bag, the more self-belief I build.

2. It means there's no plan B.

Declaring my goals out loud doesn't mean I have everything figured out yet. But saying it is the moment I stop leaving the door open for excuses, and start getting serious about the goal.

Since I know that if I say something, it's happening, I've eliminated plan B in my mind. That's important because your mind will tell you that plan B is the best way to go. When pursuing the goal is the only option, my thoughts and actions naturally align with achieving it.

3. It invites accountability and support.

You might think keeping your goal to yourself will save you from external stress, but it also means you miss out on support. Saying your goal out loud invites people to rally around you, which is good, because you'll need them.

When I told the CEO of the Princeton Club, my fitness community, and my family about my record attempt, I immediately felt like this wasn't just *my* goal anymore. Others were on board to cheer me on and help me maintain momentum, even when my own belief wavered. I was no longer alone in this.

What do you need to do to officially "commit" to your goal? Maybe it's saying it out loud to someone you trust or putting a date on your calendar that makes it real. Don't worry about the full process yet, just take one action that signals to your mind: *I'm in.*

Over time, the steps you take that prove your commitment will change how you see yourself. This isn't about being a "runner" or a "record breaker" or attaching yourself to any particular label. The most important shift is becoming someone who follows through. That's the identity that makes big goals possible. And the only way to build it is to *just start.*

Becoming "the Kind of Person"

A common misconception about big goals is that you *already* need to be the kind of person who can achieve them. But that's backwards. The truth is, you become that person through the process of pursuing the goal.

When I set out to break the world record, I wasn't yet "the kind of person" who could plank for five hours. I became that person over months of training—thousands of minutes holding the plank position, countless days nursing busted elbows, testing gear, refining my technique, and learning what my body needed. I earned that identity by showing up and doing uncomfortable things again and again, until finally, I woke up on the day of my attempt, ready to own it.

The same thing happened when I got my job as the VP of sales. I didn't feel ready to own that role. I remember holding my new business card, looking at the words Vice President, and thinking, *This doesn't feel like me.* I'd laugh as I introduced myself as the Vice President, like, "Well, that's what the card says…" But the more I stepped into the role and made decisions like a leader, the more the title started to fit. Over time, I became the kind of person who could say "I'm the VP of Sales" with confidence.

You don't become the person who achieves your goal by waiting until you feel ready. You do so by showing up anyway and letting your mind and body catch up over time.

Following through on your goals is a muscle built through repetition. So is choosing the safer path. If you've wanted to run a marathon for years, but whenever it rains, you sleep in instead of training, you've reinforced the identity of someone who lets themselves off the hook. If that's you, the feeling of regret might be just as familiar. The good news is, regret can be a useful tool.

It's a reminder that short-term comfort isn't worth the long-term disappointment.

You can use this information to make a different choice.

Show yourself that short-term discomfort *is* well worth the long-term reward.

Every time you lace up your shoes and run instead of sleeping in, even if it's just one mile, you tell yourself, *I follow through.* You'll gain something each time you do this: the satisfaction of progress, insight from what didn't go smoothly, or a little more trust that you're becoming someone who shows up. These small choices lead to big identity shifts.

The more you practice this courage, the more natural it becomes. Recently, we were on a family trip to Canada when my son, Kole, decided he wanted to go cliff jumping. He was nervous as he peered over the cliff's edge. It took him a while to work up the nerve, but once he finally jumped, he loved the feeling so much that he ran back up and did it four more times.

That's what happens when you lean into fear instead of backing away: Confidence builds through action. You realize you're capable of doing what you want, even when it feels terrifying, and you start to crave that growth. The satisfaction you feel on the other side is a reward you'll never get tired of earning.

You've already declared that you don't want to be on the comfortable road anymore. It's why you're reading this book. You want more from life. Don't worry about everything it will take to get there. Just keep showing up. Act like the person you want to become until one day, it doesn't feel like pretending anymore.

Be Here, Not There

One of the hardest parts of working toward a big goal is resisting the urge to jump too far ahead. You start imagining everything that could go wrong in the future instead of focusing on what needs your attention today.

When I was training for the plank record, I focused on the future more often than I'd like to admit. I'd think, *If I'm adding twenty minutes to my plank this week, what time does that mean I'll need to hit three weeks from now?* My brain would spiral into a future I wasn't ready for yet. But every time, I had to pull myself back to the present:

Be here, not there. *You're preparing to be* there *by showing up here today.*

I didn't need to dwell on the future. The present was where there was work to be done. The longer I held the plank, the more issues I had to troubleshoot. When I cramped up, I realized I needed to take electrolytes more seriously. When my back complained, I incorporated more pushups and rowing to strengthen my upper body.

Then came the elbow problem. My skin started splitting open from friction, and nothing seemed to help. I tried softer mats, but they made me slip more. I tried wrapping my forearms in bandages, but they twisted into tourniquets as my arms slid and swelled. Once I figured out that a firm mat and simple medical bandage worked best, there'd be something else to address, like the numbness in my feet.

I couldn't have predicted any of this. The path revealed itself as I walked it.

You won't know if your plan is solid until you put it to the test. Today's reps will teach you what works and what needs tweaking tomorrow. The more ambitious the goal, the more time you'll need to assess, adapt, and recalibrate.

I always say that your chances of success in any undertaking can be measured by your belief in yourself, but that's something that develops with time. It's something you build little by little, every time you show up.

You don't need the kind of self-belief today that will carry you across the finish line. You just need enough to start. As you progress, you'll begin to trust the process and yourself more. Instead of letting your mind spiral, your experiences become evidence to back you up. When doubts come up, like, *What if I'm not ready? What if this is too big?* you can answer them with confidence:

"It's fine. I'll be ready."

When your mind races ahead, come back to what you can do today. Just start there. Trust yourself to handle roadblocks as they come.

Chapter 3

Chapter 3

OVERCOMING ROADBLOCKS

Fear says, "Stay safe."
Doubt says you're not enough.
Failure says, "Give up."
But here's the deeper truth:
Fear means you care.
Doubt means you want this.
Failure means you're learning.
Don't let your inner voice sabotage you.
Let it prove you're on the right path.

—

The first time I stood in front of a fitness class, mic strapped to my head, thirty pairs of expressionless eyes staring back at me, I wanted to run.

This was a moment I'd been excited about for months while working toward my training certification. These were my first students, but they looked bored, maybe even annoyed, like they'd been forced to show up. My mind started racing: *They don't want to be here. They don't want me to train them. I'm going to screw this up.*

But instead of running away, I shut down those thoughts, dodged eye contact, and did what I needed to get through the hour. When we wrapped up our stretches, I thought, *Great, we all survived, but they clearly hate me. There's no way they want to take my class again.*

Then, one by one, people started walking up to thank me. Some even asked when I'd be teaching again. I thought, *Really? You didn't smile once through that entire class. You didn't look like you enjoyed any of this.*

To my surprise, that kept happening. Training sessions would start with blank stares and end with excitement. My classes kept filling up, and I had repeat students week after week.

My mind had lied to me.

I thought I was getting a "bad vibe" from my class, but really, I had misread the room. That was fear trying to protect me from a situation I'd never been in before. I mistook silence for judgment, when really it was me projecting my self-doubt onto the people around me.

I was just uncomfortable. And if I'd let discomfort convince me that teaching wasn't right for me, I would've missed the chance to discover how much I love leading fitness classes. Instead, I kept facing my fears and doubts, and standing in front of my class got a little easier each time. Of course, I screwed up, but the more I did, the more I realized screwing up is fine. It doesn't mean I'm the worst instructor ever. It means I'm human.

I'm my own worst critic, and I bet you are too. The expectations you think people have of you are rarely as heavy as the ones you pile onto yourself. Avoiding the scary thing won't quiet the inner voice that tells you you're not enough. The only thing that will quiet that voice is to keep going. Keep adding to your "bag of proof" that you are competent, you can do this, and the things you fear are often not as scary as you thought.

It's the same in other parts of life. Learning to drive is daunting at first, but after years on the road, you barely think about it. Starting a new job can be overwhelming, but a few months in, the responsibilities that once felt impossible become routine. As a parent, having your first child is terrifying too, but by the time you get to the third kid, you stop sweating every tiny detail. You realize your kids will be fine.

Discomfort and fear just mean you're in the growth zone—the *right* place to be if you want to push yourself and make big things happen in life. The good thing about this is that when you're growing, what feels unbearable today will eventually become your new normal. They're called growing pains for a reason. Trust that discomfort as a temporary, yet necessary, part of moving toward the person you want to become.

But here's what you have to watch out for: Discomfort has a funny way of disguising itself as intuition. It tries to convince you that it's your "inner voice," saying that you don't really want the goal you're working toward after all. When I stood in front of that first fitness class, everything in my mind told me I didn't want to be there—that I should just leave before I embarrassed myself. In reality, I'd spent months preparing for that moment. I wanted it more than anything.

So, how do you know when to override those thoughts and keep going anyway? How can you recognize the difference between real danger and a false alarm?

That's what this chapter is about: the ways your brain can trick you into pulling away when you should really *lean in* to achieve the growth you're looking for. With the right tools, you can get your mind working *with* you instead of against you, so you can keep moving toward your goal.

Your Sidekick for the Big Stuff: Imposter Syndrome

In Chapter 2, I mentioned that when I was promoted to VP of Sales, it took me a long time to own that title. The truth is, I felt more like an imposter during my first weeks in that role than ever before in my life. I didn't believe I deserved or truly earned it.

I started at the company as Director of Market Access. I was proud, challenged, and good at my job. But not long after I joined, the VP and CEO were let go, and suddenly the company needed to fill those gaps. I kept my head down and focused on my work, never imagining I'd be part of that conversation, until the new CEO pulled me aside.

"Before I ask the board's permission to promote you," he asked, "would you even want this?"

I was a deer in headlights. My first thought wasn't, *Yes, I can do this.* It was, *Wow, how did I fool him?* I assumed that if I took the role, he'd eventually figure out I wasn't the right person.

But in that same moment, I also felt excited. And I've learned to pay attention to that mix—excited and scared in the same breath usually means you're standing at the edge of growth. So I said yes.

Then came the hard part: quieting the voice in my head that was still whispering that I was unqualified. In those first few weeks, that inner voice tried to tell me it was a matter of time before the CEO "found me out" as a fraud and replaced me.

In the past, I might have spiraled, but instead, I looked for one objective fact I could focus on: Everyone in the company agreed that our new CEO was a smart, no-nonsense person. He wouldn't promote me if he didn't think I could thrive in this role.

That helped, so I looked for more facts I could use to override the thoughts imposter syndrome was throwing my way. I made a list of my strengths, weaknesses, and real steps I could take to feel more confident in my new role.

Fact Number 1: I was good at thinking strategically. The new CEO cited this strength as a reason he chose me for the VP role.

Fact Number 2: I'd never managed a multimillion-dollar budget before. But there were people in the organization I could lean on for advice. I made plans to meet with them and wrote out the skills I'd need to develop to feel confident with this part of the job.

Fact Number 3: I felt confident leading teams. I loved this part of my director role, and my team members enjoyed having me as a leader too.

Fact Number 4: I was inexperienced when it came to presenting at board meetings. I'd never seen public speaking as my strongest skill, but that was a matter of practice. I made a point to get in front of more rooms to get speaking reps in.

I continued like this, swapping my worries with facts, and then meeting each fact with an action I could take to develop the skill or achieve the outcome I wanted.

This is what I recommend for you too. If you have imposter syndrome working toward a big goal, you won't overcome it by waiting for the fear to disappear. Instead, start by chunking down your reality into facts and action steps:

- What skills do you need to learn to achieve this?
- What current strengths do you have that will help you get there?
- What's the most important thing to do or learn first, and what can wait?

Imposter syndrome is always with you for the scary stuff. Even people in advanced roles feel it. The main difference is that they don't let it stop them. They feel that fear and excitement in the same breath and decide to take the next step anyway. They trust themselves to figure things out as they go, and over time, that self-trust leads to confidence.

If you feel like an imposter, don't see it as a sign to quit. You've just found a dream worth pursuing. The more you lean into that discomfort, the sooner you'll be able to say, without hesitation, "I earned this. I belong here."

Roadblocks vs. Stop Signs

Not every hard thing is an obstacle meant to be overcome. Some are signals to keep pushing, and others are stop signs telling you it's time to pivot. That's okay. Sometimes, admitting something just didn't work out is the best thing for you. It gives you an opportunity to learn and a chance to find a better path.

This happened in my first marriage. There was a stop sign in front of me, but at first, I saw it as a roadblock. He was a good person; he just had a drinking problem. Everything else about our life together was great, so I thought if I supported him, we'd eventually get past this.

But that wasn't up to me. Despite counseling, conversations, and repeated attempts to move forward, things only got worse. When he started lying to me, I finally had to admit the truth: This wasn't a scary obstacle to confront and overcome. It was time for my marriage to end.

It's important to recognize when pushing forward is no longer the wisest choice. Leaving my marriage may have felt like giving up, but that decision was the right move for me and my family.

The same principle applies elsewhere. You may have to quit a sport you love to heal an injury. You may need to change your career because the role you thought you'd love is making you miserable. Sometimes the bravest decision isn't to keep fighting, but to acknowledge when it's time to redirect.

You may see experiences like these as failures, but the time you spent trying wasn't a waste. Mistakes, failure, and things simply not working out are the greatest builders of mental toughness. When you go through the next hard thing, you have proof that you've survived worse—like "failure callouses" that make you more resilient. You can look in the mirror and say, "I've been here before. It sucks, but I know what I need."

My divorce helped me see later setbacks, like losing my VP role when the company went out of business, with less self-judgment and more perspective. I wasn't as hard on myself and had a stronger belief in myself to get through it.

The question isn't whether you'll hit mental roadblocks when working toward a big goal—*you will*. And if you've never truly failed before, those first ones will hit hard. But the more you experience, the stronger your callouses become. The sting doesn't last as long, and you get better at discerning between a roadblock to push past and a stop sign telling you to pause and pivot. Here are a few questions that can help you make that distinction:

1. Is this within my control?

If the obstacle depends on someone else's choices, like my ex-husband's drinking, it may not be something you can push past. It may be a stop sign.

2. Is this helping me grow, or just hurting me?

It's okay to feel tension, but pay attention to pain. That's important when it comes to stretching muscles *and* expanding your comfort zone. Discomfort that helps you grow is worth pushing through. Pain that causes you mental or physical harm is a stop sign.

3. What's the pattern?

Look at where you've gotten stuck in the past. Have you been here before? If the same struggle keeps coming back into your life with no progress, it may be time to redirect.

The answers aren't always simple, but pausing to ask these questions can provide a valuable perspective. It moves you out of self judgment and into problem solving—an important shift to get your mind working in your favor.

The Internal Tug-of-War

Another way to get your mind on board with big goals is to become an observer of the tug-of-war between your body and mind. If you've ever had an experience like *wanting* to be consistent with fitness yet struggling to get yourself off the couch, you know what I mean. It's frustrating to feel this resistance in yourself, but if you sit with it and really notice what's going on, you can use this experience to your advantage.

Because here's the truth: Your mind can change your body, but your body can also change your mind.

For example, you might set out to run a marathon but want to quit in the first mile because your *body* complains. That's when your *mind* has to step in and say, *Keep going.* On the other hand, your *mind* might resist going to the gym, but once you get there and start moving, your body says, *Thank you. That wasn't so bad. I want to do it again.* That's your *body* changing your *mind.*

This tug-of-war can work for you or against you.

If you want to practice public speaking, your palms might sweat and your voice might shake. Your body's fight or flight mode tries to tell you to run for the hills. *This sucks. Actually, this feels dangerous. Just turn around and leave. Tell them you got sick.* But your mind knows you want this, and you'll be fine. So the mind wins that round.

During my plank training, there were days when my mind tried to tell me to quit early. *No one will even know if you get up before the third hour. You deserve a break. You have so much other stuff to do today.* But I could feel in my body that I had more left in the tank. There was no excuse not to hit my target time. So I let my body win on those days.

Some days your body is strong, but your mind is tired. Other days, your mind is determined, but your body resists. The key is awareness.

Is your body or your mind more aligned with your goals today?

Leverage the one that's stronger to get the other on board with your plan.

Getting Your Mind on the Same Page

Outsmarting the inner voice that wants to pull you back to comfort doesn't have to be a complicated process. Sometimes it's as simple as changing your language.

Let's say you're one of my wellness coaching clients and you come to me and say, "I want to lose twenty pounds." My first step isn't mapping out your training program. It's changing your words.

You have to turn that *want* into *I need, I have,* or *I can.*

This may seem small, but it's important. Because you can *say* you want something without your mind truly accepting it as a goal. So, we have to move you away from thoughts like, *It'd be nice if I could do that,* and toward, *I need this.*

From there, I'd ask *why* you need it. This is where the work to find your "why" from chapter 1 comes into play. Look at the difference:

"I want to lose 20 pounds."

versus

"I have to lose 20 pounds so I can keep up with my grandkids."

The second statement tells me this is a real priority for you, not just a dream. It says that you're more likely to show up for our training sessions, even when you're tired, it's cold and rainy, or life got busy.

Self-doubt will always lurk in the background, so you have to own your goals through your words and your actions. You can't just *kind of* do the scary thing. You can't be one foot in, one foot out.

This is true for big goals *and* difficult times, like going through my divorce. Changing the way I thought and spoke about myself made a huge difference. I told myself, *I'm not just going to be a single mom. I'm going to be the best single mom possible. I'm not ashamed of this. I made the right decision for my family.*

Of course, a big part of me was still thinking, *God, I hope I can do this. I have a toddler and another baby on the way. I don't even know what raising two children will look like yet.* So I was faking it until I made it, even internally to myself.

But repeating the identity I wanted to own, over and over, eventually made me believe it. And that's the point: Your language shapes your identity. Changing your words is an important step in changing your mind, and changing your mind is how you change your reality.

Breathing Through Roadblocks

When I teach *tree pose* in my yoga classes, students lift one foot and place it against the inside of the opposite leg, hands in prayer over their heart. We stay in the pose for a few breaths to practice balance, and then return that foot to the floor. Afterward, I'll often say, "If you feel like you're short of breath right now, you were holding your breath in the pose," and I usually hear some guilty chuckling.

We all have this tendency to brace ourselves when we face something new, challenging, or scary. For example, when riding a roller coaster, you may close your eyes and hold your breath as you approach a big drop. But you can't get as much out of that experience if you spend it bracing yourself for the worst. You miss the fun, the lessons, and the growth opportunities.

As with balanced yoga poses, the best thing you can do is breathe through challenges that come up when you pursue a big goal. You're going to wobble. You might even fall. That's fine. Uncomfortable doesn't mean unsafe.

If you're holding your breath, you're holding yourself back.

Try to remember this when you encounter mental hurdles on this journey toward your goal. You don't have to fight your way through everything. Try breathing and embracing the process. Give in to the expansion.

Breathing in and out through the hard parts, whether they're physical or mental, reminds you that you're okay, that you can keep going, and that this moment is temporary. Every time you do that, you build your self-trust and your tolerance for discomfort. You prove to yourself that you can handle more than you thought, and you carry that proof with you to the next challenge.

That's how you train your mind to choose growth over safety. Find the tools that help you show up when you're scared, so you prove to yourself, over and over, that you're stronger than your fears.

Chapter 4

EMBRACE THE PRESSURE

The world will judge and expect. That's okay.
Don't let the pressure pin you down. Let it push you forward.
Remind yourself of other times you've been
this scared and overwhelmed.
Life has been hard on you, but you've
always made it through.
Trust that you can survive this too.

—

I was thirteen when I walked into science class and saw my teacher holding up a picture of me in the local newspaper. That was the day I suddenly went from "normal kid" to the "town runner."

In my family, my brother was the hockey player, my sister was the smart one, and I was just…average. I didn't really have a "thing," so I decided to join the cross-country team. I didn't know if I was any good at running, but my friend was on the team and encouraged me to tag along. In our small town, you didn't even have to try out. They just needed enough of us to show up to pull a team together.

At first, I felt neutral about the sport. Practices were tough, and Mr. Robertson, the science teacher who served as our coach, wasn't exactly warm or encouraging.

But then I ran my first race.

I took my place at the starting line, hoping only that I could keep up with the other competitors. Instead, I crossed the finish line near the front. Race after race, I kept surprising myself and started bringing home more first-place medals. By the time I won the district meet, running wasn't just a way to have fun with friends anymore. It felt like it was my job to get better and better to make my town proud.

Even Mr. Robertson, who had hardly spoken to me before, started to notice me. When he read the front page article about my district meet win aloud in science class, the attention felt good. Like I'd finally found my "thing." But with that came more pressure than I'd ever experienced before.

External pressure isn't a bad thing. It can feel heavy, but it can also be a reason you show up when you'd rather quit. Pressure can give you the discipline and accountability you need to do incredible things. But if you're not careful, it can get the best of you. It can cause you to spiral, push yourself too hard, or even lose yourself when things don't go as planned.

When External Pressure Becomes Too Much

That pressure to meet the town's expectations got me out of bed early for cross country practice and kept me disciplined in ways I wouldn't have been on my own. My confidence grew, and I felt proud of my achievements. But as a teenager, I was new to pushing myself in this way. I didn't know the difference between pushing myself forward and pushing myself too far.

I started overtraining. After practice, I went home and ran more because I assumed more was always better. I thought that if I just put in more work, I could maintain my advantage, win more races, and make my coach, my team, and my family proud. When my legs ached, I shoved ice packs into my legwarmers, went to sleep, and got back to training the next day.

At fifteen, I finally hit my limit. I was in the middle of a race, legs pumping beneath me, sweat rolling down my neck, when suddenly, something snapped. I collapsed and couldn't get back up to finish the course. My parents rushed me to urgent care, where the doctor said I'd done enough damage to my Achilles tendon that I needed surgery.

She told me, "Once you injure your Achilles tendon to this level, you may not be able to run long distances again. You're young, so we'll see. But for now, your running days are done."

I was crushed. Just like that, the identity I'd built was taken from me, and my worst fear was realized: I felt like I'd disappointed the whole town. Everyone around me was supportive, but I couldn't shake the feeling that I'd gone from hero to zero. Mr. Robertson, who once bragged about me to the whole class, seemed to stop noticing me again. I'm sure he didn't mean it that way, but that's how it felt.

I tried to support the team from the sidelines as a coaching assistant, but it was even more painful to stand by and watch. Without running, I didn't know who I was anymore, so I was suddenly thrust into a journey of figuring that out.

When you start listening to pressure more than to yourself, it can throw you off the path to achieving a big goal. You already know that I'm a proponent of going *as hard as you can* in pursuit of your goals—fully emptying your tank. If outside pressure helps you do that, that's great.

But notice that I said *as hard as you can.* There's a difference between pressure that pushes you and pressure that shuts you off from yourself. When the noise of the world drowns out important signals from your own mind and body, you can go from feeling ahead to facing major setbacks.

Don't ignore cues like:

- Sleep deprivation (rest and recovery are crucial, not inconvenient)
- Pain (not just tension or discomfort, but pain that signals real injury)
- Prolonged stress (when the goal feels fueled by fear rather than desire)

I could have blamed my coach or the community for pushing me too far. But at the end of the day, it's up to each of us to decide how we respond to external pressure. I could have listened to the pain in my legs before I got to the point of injury.

I could have paid attention to the fact that I was pushing myself harder out of fear of letting others down.

This experience taught me early on that when it comes to pursuing big goals, more isn't always better. Smarter is better.

When you feel expectations building, pause and ask yourself: Is this pressure driving me in a healthy way, or are my actions fueled by fear and anxiety? Am I using external opinions and support to stay disciplined, or am I letting them push me past what's sustainable?

Learning to spot that difference and take ownership of how you respond—that's how you start using pressure to your advantage.

How Pressure Helps

After my injury took me out of high school cross country, I was desperate to find something to fill the void. When I lost running, I lost the physical outlet that had gotten me through the previous few years. I missed the runner's high that came from pushing my body into that breathless, anaerobic state. I missed how running added structure and discipline to my days. Most of all, I missed the sense of purpose it gave me.

So I went looking for a new outlet, but my options weren't great. First of all, I was recovering from a serious injury and surgery on my Achilles tendon. I also lived in a small town in the '80s, so I didn't have access to a gym or home workout equipment. We had Jane Fonda, but she couldn't keep me accountable the way my coach and cross-country team had. Then there were the long, brutal Minnesota winters to contend with.

So I narrowed it down to the only thing that seemed possible: indoor swimming.

I went so far as to hire a lifeguard so I could swim laps in the morning before school. It may seem like an extreme thing for a teenager to do, but that's how big the void felt at the time. Hiring a lifeguard turned out to be the perfect way to keep myself disciplined. I was paying him, and he was waiting for me, so if I said I'd be there, I had to show up.

This is a pattern woven through my life all the way to my planking challenge. It was yet another extreme endeavor, but after losing my job, there was a huge gap that was affecting me mentally. So I used the external pressure of announcing my world record attempt and setting a date for it to give me purpose in that season.

Pressure from the outside world has many advantages. You just need to know how to leverage them. It can keep you accountable to your goals. It can help you build the good habits you want for yourself. It can also show you opportunities to become *more* than you might not recognize on your own.

When I joined cross-country, I didn't dream of being a standout runner. I was just happy to be on the team. But when my coach and community noticed my talent, I got a chance to see what I was made of. Despite the outcome, I see that experience as a win, because it revealed a level of determination that I didn't know I had. The lessons I learned shaped how I've approached challenges for the rest of my life.

Something similar happened in my career when I was promoted to my role as the VP of Sales. Suddenly, the whole company was leaning on me. That was a lot of pressure, but it also gave me the opportunity to rise to the occasion, develop new skills, and prove to myself I could lead at a level I'd never envisioned.

That's the upside of pressure. It can help you grow into a version of yourself you didn't know existed. The key is checking in with yourself and asking: *Do I actually want to take this on? Does this opportunity align with who I want to become? I may feel scared, but do I feel excited too?* When the answer is yes, embracing the pressure can lead to better outcomes than you could have imagined.

Owning Your Truth in Public

Now I'm a divorced person. That's a fun title.

After my first marriage ended, I had to redefine myself again. This time, it wasn't an exciting goal I was moving toward, but external expectations affected me all the same.

I couldn't afford a new house yet because I was still locked into my old mortgage, and the divorce process, especially with kids involved, takes time. So, as a newly single mom with a toddler and a baby on the way, I moved us back to the small town where I was once a star runner, to live with my parents.

I was grateful to have their support, but I was also disappointed in myself. I kept thinking, *This is not where I should be in my life.*

My hometown is the kind of place where word spreads fast. People were friendly and curious about my life. But when you're already feeling vulnerable, even innocent comments can feel like judgment. I could practically hear the whispers:

"Rashelle's back in town!"

"Is she visiting?"

"I saw her last week. I wonder how long she'll be here."

I got tired of dodging questions. So one day, I decided to rip off the bandage. Let the grapevine spread the news. They can do all the talking they want, and then we can move on.

I was headed to the public library, my maternity shirt billowing in front of me and my toddler kicking her feet in the stroller, when a woman I knew stopped to chat with me. She asked how long I was visiting, and I was finally honest:

"I'm not visiting. I'll be here for a while. I'm going through a divorce."

In that moment, my narrative shifted from, "God, I failed," to "judge all you want—this is my reality." It was a really tough time in my life, but hiding it only kept me stuck. Owning it was a key step in moving forward.

Whether you're setting a big goal or going through a challenging season, change allows you to choose a new identity. It's easier to share a win than something you see as a failure, but once you put it out there, you'll experience a strong sense of relief. Humans aren't meant to go through challenges alone. Telling people what you're up against right now may feel like opening yourself up to judgment, but you're also opening the door to receive the support you need to get through this.

Making Pressure Your Ally

When external pressure gets to you, try using this reframe: *You should want to feel uncomfortable, even want people to judge you, because it means you're doing something outside the ordinary.* Try not to dwell on what others think. You can't control that anyway. Instead, focus on what their reactions represent: You're stepping into new territory to achieve something big. Let that motivate you on tough days.

There will be times when your best move *isn't* to grit your teeth and accept the voices or environment around you. Sometimes, the smartest way to get external pressure on your side is to change the inputs in your life: your environment, your people, and what you feed your mind.

When I started training for my world record attempt, planking at home made it easier to stick with my schedule. But as I increased my time, training alone in the dark at 4:00 a.m. while my family slept made the hours drag. So I moved my training to the gym.

It was still 4:00 a.m., but inside the gym, it could have been 4:00 p.m. The lights were bright, people were running and lifting weights, and the energy was high. Suddenly, I wasn't training alone. As members found out what I was doing, they'd plank with me for a few minutes or just stretch out next to me to chat and pass the time. On a hard day, someone might stop to say I inspired them, and that encouragement would fill me up enough to keep going.

The same was true after my cross-country injury, when I started swimming before school. Most teenagers wouldn't hire a lifeguard so they could wake up early to swim, but that choice gave me the accountability I needed to move forward. And when I went through my divorce, moving back home was hard, but it gave me new surroundings, which made it easier for me to step into my new identity as a single mother of two.

You can apply this to any big goal or challenge you have in front of you. Look at the environment, people, and other external inputs influencing your life. Assess what's helping you move toward your goal and what might need to change.

For example, if you want to lose twenty pounds, put yourself in spaces that support that goal. Connect with like-minded people working toward similar goals. Surround yourself with healthy foods you actually enjoy. Unfollow social media accounts that make you feel inadequate, or swap scrolling for videos, podcasts, and books that inspire you.

So much of life isn't up to us, but one thing you *can* control is how you respond to pressure. Ask yourself: *What can I reconfigure in my life to make reaching this goal easier? How can I align my surroundings with the person I'm becoming?*

Look at the inputs you can control so your environment acts as an ally, helping you stay disciplined, reach your goals, and seize opportunities to get more out of life.

Chapter 5

CONTROL WHAT YOU CAN

---

*The alarm goes off, but **you** have to wake up.*
*The gym is open 24/7, but **you** have to show up.*
*The job is posted, but **you** have to apply.*
Opportunities come. So do setbacks.
You can't control either.
But you can control how you respond.
Own that, and create your own success.

—

"Hey," a fellow Amazon driver motioned for me to roll down my window. When I did, he leaned out of his own truck with a curious look on his face. "Everyone's been asking me this… Are you an *Undercover Boss*?"

He must have asked because I didn't seem to belong there. Maybe I was too upbeat, smiling in the cold when everyone else was grinding through their shifts. Evidently, I stood out so much that it felt more likely that I was secretly evaluating them—not really there to deliver packages.

I laughed, "I'm not, I swear!"

He chuckled and joked that he didn't believe me.

I took it as a compliment. Losing my job as Vice President of Sales and ending up as an Amazon delivery driver could have been a low point in my career. I could have shown up bitter, done the bare minimum, collected the paycheck, and kept feeling sorry for myself. Instead, I decided to approach this job with the same positive attitude I brought to my VP role.

Delivering packages in the dead of winter is hard. But I told myself, *You have to look for the silver lining here. You have to make this job fun. Because if you don't, you're going to hate it, and you'll get angrier about your circumstances.*

So that's what I did. I went into every shift trying to find purpose in the work I was doing. I joked with my coworkers while we waited for our trucks to be loaded. I wore a Santa hat to deliver packages around the holidays. I laughed with customers, carried their boxes in when they needed a hand, and thanked them for the snacks they offered to help me get through my workday.

At the end of a shift, I didn't come home and mope about being overqualified for the job or missing my warm VP office. I checked my Amazon app to see how customers ranked my services, and celebrated the five-star ratings that came in.

If you belittle the work, you belittle yourself.

That's what I kept telling myself. Because it didn't really matter what my job title was. It didn't matter that the work was backbreaking or that my skillset would've been better suited to a different role. This was just another uncomfortable situation I found myself in. I wasn't going to be in it forever, but I *was* in it now. So all I could control was the mindset I brought to each shift. I could let it give me the purpose I needed during that time. I could treat this job like it mattered, because it did.

Working as a delivery driver taught me a life lesson that proved crucial in my plank training: Your sense of control can be your greatest advantage or your greatest trap.

There are so many uncontrollable variables influencing each of us at any given time: the economy, the job market, your current title, other people's opinions, the timing of opportunities, and even things like the weather or how well you slept last night. If you spend your energy trying to control the uncontrollable, you'll drive yourself into frustration. With this line of thinking, you may even give up or decide not to try in the first place.

So the best approach is to zero in on what's truly yours to own: your mindset, your effort, and your response to the circumstances and tasks you face today. That's how you build the resolve to move forward, no matter what's happening around you. That's how you endure discomfort, and regardless of the outcome, find a way to win anyway.

Focus on the controllables and let go of the rest. It's easier said than done, but this skill is essential for building the mental toughness to pursue your biggest goals.

Focus on Today

When my plank training times got longer, I started looking for stories to distract my mind and help me burn down the clock. I didn't crave fiction or fantasy; I wanted to hear about people overcoming hardship to achieve great things. Popping in my earbuds and listening to books like *Can't Hurt Me* by David Goggins became an essential part of my training regimen.

Each of the stories I consumed helped fortify my mindset as I prepared for my world record attempt. But one in particular stayed with me as the perfect example of controlling what you can: former US Senator John McCain's experience as a prisoner of war (POW) during the Vietnam War.

John McCain was shot down in Hanoi, Vietnam, while serving as a Navy pilot.[1] He spent the next five and a half years in Hoa Lo Prison, enduring severe torture, isolation, heat exhaustion, malnutrition, dysentery, and injuries that resulted in permanent disabilities, never knowing if or when his suffering would end.

That's what struck me the most about McCain's story: his mental toughness to face each day when there was no end date and no guarantee he'd make it out alive.

He didn't give up, either. He found ways to move when he could, and he and his fellow prisoners even developed a tapping code to encourage each other through the walls.

---

1 "McCain Institute Commemorates 30 Years of Normalized Relations Between U.S. and Vietnam," McCain Institute, July 11, 2025, https://www.mccaininstitute.org/resources/press-releases/commemorating-30-years-of-normalized-relations-between-us-and-vietnam.

Stories like this fueled me because, by comparison, my plank training was nothing. Even when I was planking for three hours or more, I always knew exactly how long was left. Watching the clock tick down gave me the energy to finish strong.

John McCain didn't have that luxury. But even without assurance that the nightmare would end, he woke up every day and focused on one thing: *Get through today.* He zeroed in on what he could control: his mindset, his response to horrific conditions, and the bonds he made with fellow POWs.

This attitude even extended to choices that could have changed everything. Because McCain's family had political connections, he was offered early release. He refused, knowing his departure would crush the hope of the other prisoners.

I remember hearing his story and thinking, *Holy cow, that's the most extreme form of mental toughness.* He couldn't control the beatings, the lack of food, or the fact that he was indefinitely trapped on the other side of the world from his family. But he could control how he showed up to face each moment as it passed. He could hold onto his integrity, find purpose in community, and push forward, even in the most dire circumstances.

That's the point: No matter what you're trying to overcome or pursue, you don't need to know how the whole journey will unfold. That's not controllable.

Even in plank training, I could see the clock counting down, and I could control how I pushed my mind and body through each session, but I couldn't see the future. I couldn't predict if

I'd get injured in three weeks, plateau in four months, or receive the official world record title from Guinness in the end.

The future wasn't mine to control. Today was.

Stop trying to control the future. Just find a way to win today. Get really clear on what you can and can't control, so you know the best place to focus your energy to move closer to your goal.

Find Your Controllables

Think about the big goal you're working toward. If it feels overwhelming, it's probably because you're worried about the countless parts of it that are outside your control. You can't control if your day gets derailed by an unexpected disaster. You can't predict other people's actions. So define what you *can* control, and rely on those controllables to build your path forward.

How do you separate the controllables from the uncontrollables? Ask yourself if you have the power to change the circumstance or setback in front of you. Here are a few examples:

> After I injured my Achilles tendon in cross-country, I couldn't keep running. That was a fact I didn't have the power to change. ***Uncontrollable.***
>
> Based on the available options, I had the power to choose swimming as a new outlet to rebuild my fitness and confidence. ***Controllable.***
>
> When my first husband struggled with drinking, I couldn't make him stop. We can't make other people's choices for them. ***Uncontrollable.***

When we couldn't make it work, I had the power to end the marriage and build a healthier life for my kids and me. ***Controllable***.

When I lost my VP job because the company closed, I couldn't control the job market, the hundreds of applicants I competed with, or the stream of rejections. ***Uncontrollable***.

I could control my actions during the job hunt: reaching out to my network, keeping a positive attitude as I delivered Amazon packages, and continuing my plank training to give myself purpose. ***Controllable***.

For your goal, notice the controllables and uncontrollables. Get clear on what *you* have the power to make happen, because the steps you need to take to reach your goal must be within your control. Yes, you'll still have to wake up in the morning and get yourself to follow through. But this way, you put the power in your own hands. As much as it possibly can be, your success is up to you.

I say "as much as it possibly can be" for an important reason: To some extent, outcomes are always uncontrollable. You can control your effort. You can control your daily actions. You can control your attitude. You can do *everything within your power* to set yourself up for success. But none of us can control exactly how things turn out.

Even when something *seems* controllable, you might need to assess it more closely. For example, if you're struggling to get out of bed for morning workouts, don't just label yourself as lazy. Look deeper: Will this continue to be an issue? To resolve it, can you control your evening routine or the time of day you train?

Life happens. Unexpected setbacks will test you. At times, *everything* in your world might feel uncontrollable. When I lost my VP job, nothing felt within my control. That's why I turned to planking: It gave me back my power. It gave me something I could control.

When the uncontrollable shows up, give yourself grace and pivot back to the controllable. Say you planned to train at the gym this morning, but you wake up to a snowstorm. Now you're snowed in and unable to complete your routine as expected.

The weather is uncontrollable. The only controllable is what you do next.

Do you tell yourself you failed because something uncontrollable prevented you from training the way you wanted to? Or do you assess your options—maybe try an equivalent workout at home or rearrange your training schedule—and accept that you did everything in your power to stick with the plan?

Uncontrollables distract the mind.

Controllables are where your only real solutions are.

Don't waste energy fighting the things you can't change. Redirect it into what's yours to own: your attitude, your daily actions, and the skills you can develop. And here's the catch: Just because you *can* control something doesn't mean you actually *will*. That's where building discipline becomes critical.

Building Discipline

When I started my VP job, I couldn't control the strengths and weaknesses I came into the role with. But I could control which skills I built from there. To pursue any big goal, one of the most important tools you need to sharpen is your discipline.

Discipline is what keeps you going when the excitement fades. External motivators like titles, awards, recognition, or reaching a certain dress size can get you started, but they're not enough to get you to the finish line. That's why we spent chapter 1 developing a deeper "why" to guide your journey.

But sometimes, even knowing what matters to you isn't enough. If this goal is bigger than anything you've attempted before, you'll likely face more discomfort than you've ever experienced. Even when you care deeply about something, there will be days when you're tired, scared, frustrated, or just don't *feel* like showing up. Discipline is what gets you to show up anyway.

Motivation is feeling. Discipline is action despite feeling.

If you only take action when you feel good, you'll never reach your goal. It wasn't fun for me to wake up at 4:00 a.m. and look at the floor for four hours during plank training. Even the thought of breaking the record wasn't enough to get me out of bed.

The reality is, we only have so much control over how we feel. You can cultivate a positive mindset and still argue with your partner, spill coffee all over yourself, or get pulled into a conflict at work that affects your mood. Motivation fluctuates based on so many factors. You can't manufacture it when it isn't there.

Motivation is uncontrollable. Discipline is controllable.

What kept me disciplined during plank training was knowing what this journey was giving me internally. Every time I fought through discomfort to complete a session, I felt proud of myself, like I could do anything. After I lost my job, I was missing that confidence. Rebuilding it mattered enough for me to take action, no matter how I felt on any given day.

The good thing is, discipline builds on itself. Every time you take action toward your goal despite discomfort, you add another contribution to your "bag of proof." You show yourself that you have the power to handle discomfort and follow through anyway.

Creating a World Where the New You Fits

The journey toward your goal will be hard, but you have some control over *how* hard. First, accept that you're not just asking yourself to pursue a goal. You're asking yourself to change your life.

Whether you're studying for a certification, learning to play the guitar, or working on your public speaking skills, the changes you're asking yourself to make are most likely not temporary. Even with something physical like running a marathon, you're going to be in this for a long period of time. So you need to make sure the steps fit into your life.

My plank training affected my day-to-day life and even my family and friends. Planking took a big slice out of my pie of time. I had to look at what I was asking of myself and my life. I had to make sure this goal wasn't requiring so much discipline that I had to put my enjoyment on pause.

I surrounded myself with people who encouraged me. I adjusted my schedule so training fit into my life rather than constantly competing with it. And I had to find tradeoffs that allowed me to have fun while living in a world where my goal could become a reality.

I cut out alcohol for four months to improve my performance, which isn't a big deal on its own, but on the lake where I live, parties and cocktails are part of the culture. At first, the change felt isolating, but I found ways to make it work. I went to the parties to see friends but left early, explaining that I had to be up at 4:00 a.m. to train. Having a clear reason helped me stick to my choice without feeling awkward, and it let me enjoy the social time without the pressure to drink.

Being too strict with yourself is a common mistake. I see it often with diet and exercise: People set a goal based on an idealistic version of life where everything goes according to plan. As a result, they force themselves into such extreme discipline that their goal starts to feel like a punishment. Too much rigidity doesn't allow for fun *or* the unpredictability of life. With this approach, you're setting yourself up to fail, blaming yourself, and entering another cycle of starting over.

Instead, get specific about the *sustainable* actions you can take. Ask yourself:

> *What can I do consistently that will help me reach my goal?*
> Example: Waking up at 4:00. a.m. for plank training was sustainable for me.

> *What am I not willing to give up?*
> Example: I needed to spend time with my kids, so I built that into the plan.
> *What can I moderate?*
> Example: I still wanted to socialize, but I wouldn't drink or stay late at parties.

Once you determine the tradeoffs your goal requires, make them gradually. Experiment with moderating your lifestyle first and keep asking yourself, *Does this feel sustainable?* As you go, you may decide it will work to cut certain habits entirely, while others are too important to eliminate.

Maybe cutting weeknight social events is harder than you thought, so you keep one early night with friends and make sure you have a lighter training session the next day. Maybe practicing guitar for two hours is unrealistic, so you switch to shorter sessions on weekdays and a longer block on Saturday.

You're building a world where the new you fits. You need to *like* it if you're going to keep living there. Take time to think through this process to set yourself up with a plan you can control *and* stick with.

Making Tomorrow-You Proud

It's normal to get frustrated by the uncontrollables in life, especially when the outcome itself—whether or not you actually achieve your goal—is uncontrollable to some degree. You can empty your tank, follow every step of your plan, and still hit obstacles that prevent you from performing as you hoped.

So don't dwell on the outcome. Don't think a dozen steps ahead. Instead, focus on tomorrow-you. You can't control exactly how you'll respond to future events, but you do know better than anyone what tomorrow-you will need to accept even the most unfavorable outcome.

On the day of my plank record attempt, I knew tomorrow-me needed to be certain that I gave everything I had. Guinness would make the final call, but my effort was mine to own. I'd trained to the best of my ability. I'd gotten myself to that big moment. At that point, the only controllable—the only thing I could do to make tomorrow-me proud—was giving it my best shot.

What will make tomorrow-you proud? Based on your past experiences, what can you control today to feel okay no matter what happens? By owning what you can today, you set tomorrow-you up to win.

PART 2

RISE AND BEGIN

Chapter 6
BABY STEPS

Don't worry about the months ahead.
Focus on surviving today.
You don't need to see the whole path. Just the next step.
Each step proves you can keep going,
And pulls a little more of your path into view.

—

When my first marriage ended, I was pregnant with my oldest son, Kyle, and chasing after my two-year-old daughter, Tyler. I was about to enter a challenging new phase that I couldn't even imagine yet: life as a single mother with two young children, sharing custody with their father.

I was on board with dual custody, but my mind spiraled anyway:

What happens when he meets another woman?

How will holidays work when they're not with me?

Will I be able to afford daycare? A mortgage?

Ten diapers a day at this price, times seven days a week, times this many months…

I'd lie awake at night doing this future-math, like these were equations I could solve if I just kept thinking. But worrying didn't reduce my worries. It multiplied them.

Eventually, a thought interrupted me:

No. We're not there yet.

Somehow, a voice of reason in my head found a way to quiet the noise. It gave me clarity on how to move forward when all the "what ifs" felt debilitating. It said:

There are so many things ahead of you that you've never done. It's impossible to know what the future looks like. You're not going to know how you'll handle any of this until it happens. Just stay here.

What do you need to do today?

Go to the doctor? Do laundry?

Just stay here.

I couldn't fix holidays five years down the road or calculate the exact budget for a baby who wasn't born yet. But I could look at my to-do list for the day ahead. I could take care of what was in front of me.

When the future feels uncertain, whether you're navigating a season of change or pursuing the biggest goal of your life, your mind can't help but race ahead. It's scanning for threats to try to protect you.

But this fixation on "solving" the future leads to analysis paralysis: when overthinking literally keeps you stuck in place. Not only is that an overwhelming and exhausting state to live in, but it rarely helps you work through the challenge you face today.

When this happens, catch yourself and pull your mind back to the present. Focus only on the step in front of you right now. That's how we'll map out the path to your big goal: not by trying to predict every possible twist or turn on your journey, but by breaking the path into manageable baby steps you can take, one at a time.

Why Baby Steps Work

When I was training for my first marathon, I wrote out my mileage progression for each week leading up to race day. As I got closer to that date, I looked at the calendar and thought, *Oh my God, twenty miles?!*

I had to bring myself back:

No. We're not there yet.

We're on week four. Week four says you're running five miles. You can do five.

That's the value of baby steps. They help shift your mind out of *that sounds impossible* thinking and into *I can do that.* Instead of letting the twenty miles send me into a spiral, I gave myself permission to focus on today's five, knowing they'd get me closer to the goal.

The same thing happened when I announced I was going to attempt to break the planking world record. The words left my mouth, and my stomach flipped, because I wasn't there yet. The record was hours beyond what I could hold at the time.

And unlike marathon training, there weren't any best practices to follow for my plank goal. Literally no one had done it before. That could've sent me into another spiral. But that's the point: I didn't need to plank for five hours the day I announced my goal. I didn't need to know exactly how I'd get there either. I just needed to show up for my next training session.

This is where many people stall out with a big goal. You don't have all the information yet, so it feels impossible. You've never done this before. Maybe no one has. Announcing your goal kicks off the spiral, and you can go one of two ways:

1. Too much future-thinking sends you into analysis paralysis.
2. Too much urgency pushes you to overdo it.

I had to fight that second trap when I became VP of Sales. I wanted to prove myself, so I felt this sense of urgency to run straight to market with our new product. But more analytical teammates pulled me back into the room with questions like "What does it cost?" and "How will it help people?"

I realized I couldn't rush this. I needed to slow down and focus on baby steps like testing messages, educating our teams, and gathering feedback. Skipping steps wouldn't lead to the success I wanted.

Big goals come with nerves, and often excitement, too. Both are *controllable* factors if you can recenter your mind on the next baby step. Like the tortoise and the hare, slow and steady wins. Baby steps are how you slow down and bring yourself back to today.

Breaking Big Goals Into Small Wins

When you're staring at a huge goal, avoid getting ahead of yourself by mapping out baby steps that are:

- Attainable
- Sustainable

Attainable baby steps don't require you to become a completely different person. They align with who you are and what your life looks like today. Are you a morning person? Build your workout routine around that. Have evenings free? That's your guitar practice slot. Attainable means realistic for *you*, not what works for someone else.

Sustainable baby steps are ones you can repeat long-term without injuring yourself, falling out of other important routines, or burning out. The idea is to turn the steps into habits, and it's easier to do that with consistent, daily action than with big actions once in a while. Working out for four hours on Saturday and skipping the rest of the week won't get you far. But twenty minutes every day will. Consistency beats intensity.

Here's how to map out your baby steps:

1. Pick a realistic date on the calendar for when you want to reach your goal.

2. Work backward to determine milestones you need to hit leading up to that date.

3. Break each milestone into the smallest possible steps that feel attainable today and are sustainable over a long period of time.

Don't overthink this or aim for the perfect plan. The one you make now won't be the exact path you'll take anyway. Just start with your best-guess baby steps.

For example:

- If your goal is to run a marathon in four months, maybe it's three miles this week, four the next, gradually building until race day.

- If your goal is to learn guitar, it could be ten minutes of practice each evening instead of one jam session a month.

- If your goal is to pay off debt, maybe it's cutting one expense this week and another next week while putting a set amount toward your balance every payday.

If your goal doesn't come with a clear roadmap, like my plank training, see that as an opportunity. It might feel intimidating at first, but creating your own steps builds confidence. When you look at the path you created, you can say, "I did that." That sense of ownership is one of the most rewarding parts of the process.

Turning It Into a System

Once you've mapped out baby steps that feel attainable *and* sustainable, the next challenge is making the process as automatic as possible. You do that by:

1. Minimizing decisions
2. Developing rituals
3. Accounting for life

Minimizing Decisions

Little decisions drain energy and create openings to talk yourself out of taking action. The more you can pre-decide, the easier it becomes to follow through.

During plank training, I never woke up wondering if I should train. I had already written my target minutes for the week on the calendar. I always looked one week ahead so I could find the best windows to plank around my plans and block off recovery time. The plan didn't have to be perfect. The decision just had to be made in advance. That way, my only job was to show up.

Treat your baby steps like the systems you already run on autopilot: your morning routine, your commute, and even the way you make your coffee. You don't question these systems; you just do them. That's what you want your baby steps to feel like. Not *I have to force myself to do this*, but *this is just what I do*.

Developing Rituals

Beyond logistics, see how else you can make your baby steps easier to take. Adding in rituals can further reduce decision fatigue and make the process more fun.

For me, planking looked like this:

- charge my phone overnight,
- stick to an early bedtime routine,
- wear a similar outfit each session,
- bring the same towel and water bottle,
- bring headphones and something motivating to listen to,
- use the same mat in the same area of the gym,
- shower right after, and
- bandage my elbows.

None of this was automatic at first. I developed these rituals over time.

These weren't superstitions, but I understand why superstitions can help. For example, in every photo of me racing, I'm in the same white hat. People must have thought it was my lucky hat, but I wore it because it kept my hair back, absorbed my sweat, and stayed put on windy days.

Over time, these repeated routines take on a sentimental quality. They help you find your comfort zone within the discomfort. Use this to your advantage. It can help turn hard work into something you look forward to repeating.

Accounting for Life

Your system can't be too rigid, because real life won't follow your "ideal" plan. Build leeway in both the short term and the long term.

On a daily level, I scheduled enough time to stretch beforehand, recover afterward, and commute both ways. On a weekly level, I made sure there were days to heal between long sessions.

Then, I built a two-week cushion into the plan. This helped me account for uncontrollables like illness, travel, or transitions throughout the year, like when my son heads back to school. Too much buffer, though, risks hitting the goal too soon. I thought back to marathon training: Once you've run 26.2 miles, you don't want to keep running that distance every week, or you'll risk injury. The same principle applies here.

Things will change as you go, but building a simple system makes showing up easier. It helps you settle into your routine, so you can focus less on deciding and more on doing.

Take a Step, Assess, Adjust, Repeat

Once I accepted that I had to invent my own training plan for the plank world record, I realized that on some level, that's what all of us are doing: making it up as we go.

Even with endless information at your fingertips, you can't anticipate how things will feel until you feel them. You can't predict which equipment will work best, how your body will respond, or which people will show up to help in unexpected ways.

So remember that your best-guess baby steps are a hypothesis. Each new step is an experiment to test that hypothesis, collect information, and use what you learn to inform your next step.

In other words, the path to your goal boils down to:

1. Take a step
2. Assess
3. Adjust
4. Repeat

For plank training, one baby step was just showing up for the day's session. Afterward, I'd assess by asking myself simple questions:

How did today go?
What felt strong?
What didn't work?
Where did I feel pain?
How can I create more support for that area?

The answers weren't reasons to quit. They were information I could use to adjust the path from there. Sometimes it was as simple as realizing my back felt weak and adding strength training to support it. I couldn't have planned that before I started; it only became clear once I was in the process.

When my progress stalled several months in, I could've decided my plan wasn't working and given up. Instead, I looked for an easy adjustment. I had planned to remove alcohol from my diet in the final month, so I decided to try cutting it sooner. Maybe it was the placebo effect, but that change seemed to help me break out of the plateau.

When you treat each day like an experiment, you can release the pressure to get everything right up front. Just take today's best-guess baby step, see how it goes, adjust, and keep moving. There's no better way to prepare for tomorrow.

When Thinking Ahead Helps

Mapping out baby steps is about focusing on today instead of drowning in "what ifs." But there *is* one way of thinking ahead that can help you: visualization.

Research shows that mentally rehearsing an activity can improve performance almost as much as physical practice.[2] Athletes use visualization all the time, and I did too in my cross-country days. Before a race, my coach had us walk the course to see the terrain. Later, I'd run it in my mind. I pictured the tricky hills, the smell of the golf course, the rhythm of my breathing, and how my body would move.

Instead of spiraling, this was like a meditation. It gave my brain something useful to do with the pressure, calmed my anxiety, and helped race day feel familiar—like I'd already been there.

I've used this tool in other areas since. When I became VP of Sales, I was nervous about board presentations, so I visualized them. I saw myself speaking with confidence, controlling my

---

2 Maamer Slimani, David Tod, Helmi Chaabene, Bianca Miarka, and Karim Chamari. "Effects of Mental Imagery on Muscular Strength in Healthy and Patient Participants: A Systematic Review," *Journal of Sports Science & Medicine* 15, no. 3 (2016): 434-450. https://pmc.ncbi.nlm.nih.gov/articles/PMC4974856/.

pace, and connecting with the people on the other side of the table.

The key is to use visualization positively. Don't picture yourself messing up or getting embarrassed. That's just letting anxiety take over. Direct your mind toward the outcome you want: the winning goal, the calm presentation, or the proud moment hiking with your family. If you can't keep it positive, stop and return to your baby steps.

If you want to try visualization, remember to:

1. Use it when you're feeling nervous about your goal.
2. Picture the sights, smells, sounds, and feelings associated with your goal.
3. Remind yourself of your "why" as you visualize your goal.
4. Keep it short. Just visualize your goal for a few minutes at a time.
5. Always visualize the outcome you want to see happen.

This is your goal for a reason. It's okay to let yourself get excited about it. Visualization can help you shift from nerves to excitement. It can remind you why you're doing this, and why the discomfort is worth enduring.

Trusting the Baby Steps

Big goals can be overwhelming. It's just part of the package. Whether you're someone who meets overwhelming goals with procrastination or, like me, you tend to overdo it, your baby steps are here to help. They remind you that you're not supposed to see the whole path before you take the first step.

Just zoom in on what's in front of you and know that the best learning happens as you go, not *before* you go.

The power of baby steps is that they build trust in yourself and in the process. Each baby step you take is proof that you can do this. As those steps add up, they help you create the confidence and establish the pace you need to reach the finish line—traits you couldn't have had at the start.

So don't pressure yourself to figure it all out today. Focus on the best-guess baby step in front of you. Then the next. Take a step, assess, adjust, repeat. One day, you'll look back and see how those small steps lined up and led you to your goal.

Want help building habits that stick?

Through one-on-one wellness coaching, I can help you create a holistic plan to work toward any big fitness or lifestyle goal. Book a free thirty-minute consultation, and we can discuss the path that'd be most supportive for you.

Visit www.riseshineco.com for coaching and speaking inquiries.

Chapter 7

YOUR DAY ONE KIT

Want to change your life? Change what you do today.
Even if your plan is imperfect, take the next right step.
Set your foundation. Become the person who shows up.
Day One is where your new identity begins.

—

Think about the last big trip you took. In the weeks beforehand, you probably planned activities, made sure you had the right clothes and documents, and packed your bags. That's what we did in the previous chapters: We "packed your bags" with the mindset shifts, tools, and proof you need to set out on Day One of the journey to your goal.

But the night before a flight, things feel more real. You double-check your ticket. You calculate how early you'll need to leave for the airport, then tack on extra time in case traffic or security slows you down. You do your best to prepare, but you can't predict everything. There might be delays. Your hotel could be under construction. You don't know how it will all play out, but that's not your job.

Now that you've prepared everything you can, your job is simple: Know what to do to make your flight. In other words, know your tomorrow.

Day One of your goal works the same way. By now, you've figured out your "why," explored your controllables and uncontrollables, and mapped out your best-guess baby steps to take next. Your bags are packed. Now it's time to go.

So before your alarm goes off on Day One, let's run through the final checks to set you up for success. Again, this doesn't mean Day One will be perfect. It means you'll have the confidence and system in place to keep moving when things get uncomfortable.

Day One is about showing up, using the tools you already have, and picking up new ones as you go. You're waking up, going through security, and getting on that plane, even with all the unknowns ahead. This is about the transition from *thinking* about your goal to *living* as the person who pursues it.

Your Weather-Proof System

Just like a trip isn't part of your everyday routine, embarking on your goal is something new. It takes extra energy to map out the details. At first, it might feel clunky because your new habits haven't become automatic yet. So here's a reframe to help.

Treat the next couple of weeks like you're taking a trip, and every day is a different leg of the journey. Some days will go smoothly. Other days, you'll hit delays or detours. But every day teaches you something new about how you "travel" best.

Say you're starting a new workout routine. Your Day One might involve trying a new fitness class, but you won't know if it's the right fit until you go. If it clicks, great! Add it to your plan for next week. If not, that's useful information too. You still took action and learned something that makes your plan stronger tomorrow.

In chapter 6, we talked about turning your baby steps into a system. This is where you start manually refining your system in real time. Let it be messy and imperfect. Each experiment adds to your knowledge until habits start to take shape. Those habits form the foundation of your "weather-proof system"— the one that keeps you steady even when you hit turbulence.

A System That Feels Like Home

Here's where some people overcomplicate this: They add unnecessary tasks into their system just because they've heard they should. This is why I'm not prescribing a one-size-fits-all regimen. Personally, I love writing to-do lists on sticky notes, but maybe you prefer your notes app or a journal. If journaling helps you, go for it. But any task that feels like punishment or busywork will weigh your system down.

That doesn't mean you should dismiss everything that feels inconvenient. Sometimes, the evidence shows that a habit you'd rather skip actually increases your odds of success. For example, many people see better fitness results when they track their food. Knowing that, you may decide it's worth doing, or you may still find it isn't for you. The point is to build a system that truly supports you, not one that forces you into someone else's mold.

Our bigger purpose here is to determine how *you* best form habits. Habit formation is the key to shifting your effort from manual to automatic. It's how you arrive at the system that helps you reach your goal.

So use Day One, and the next few weeks, to take messy action and observe what happens. Notice what works and what feels heavy, and keep adjusting from there.

Here are some questions that can help make sure you're ready for Day One:

- What's the best-guess baby step you can take tomorrow? Is it a fitness class? A one-mile run? A piano lesson?
- What tools or reminders will help you follow through?
- Can you lay out your clothes or pack a bag the night before?
- Do you need to set your alarm for a certain time?
- Do you need to adjust your evening routine so you have enough energy?
- What are you hoping to learn by taking this step?
- What will you gain even if things don't go as you hope?
- Which steps can you see *turning into* consistent, automatic routines you just wake up and do?

Again, the goal here isn't perfection. It's getting to the point where, if someone asks, "What are you doing tomorrow?" you already have an answer. You don't have to think because the decision is made. The bag is packed. The itinerary is set.

Over time, you'll form habits that help shortcut your progress. You'll stand in the same spot during your favorite fitness class. You'll find the route you always take to the basketball court. Your system becomes that specific, and details that once felt like effort become second nature.

And when life inevitably throws you off with holidays, travel, sick kids, or just a bad day, the system you're building gives you something to get back to. Just like coming home from vacation, slipping back into a well-formed routine feels grounding.

That's why you want a system you actually like. Even though pursuing your goal comes with discomfort, the system that gets you there shouldn't feel like punishment. Eventually, it should feel as automatic and natural as possible, like returning home.

Your Day One Team

One of the biggest barriers people face ahead of Day One has nothing to do with preparation. It's guilt.

If you're always giving your time to others, you may feel like you have to "ask permission" to go after your own goal. That martyr mindset convinces you it's selfish to carve out time for yourself. But here's the truth:

1. You deserve to go after what you want in life. Period.
2. You're not stealing from loved ones. You're investing in the person they rely on.
3. If they're really your people, they *want* to help you. You just have to let them.

If you're going on a trip, you may ask a friend to look after your dog or water the plants. You don't feel guilty asking for that help—that's what communities are for. The same applies to pursuing your goal.

On my world record attempt day, my system broke down. My arm went numb—I hit turbulence I hadn't planned for and needed help. So I asked my neighbor, Andy, to tell me about his time in Iraq. His story helped me find the strength to keep going when my body and mind wanted to quit. If I hadn't brought my people along for my training journey, I wouldn't have had Andy's support to lean on that day.

Andy wouldn't want me to feel guilty for needing his help. If anything, the opposite would be true. A good support system would be upset to know they could've helped you achieve something, but you were too afraid to ask.

So identify the people who could be there for you on this journey, and give yourself permission to ask them for help. Maybe you want to take an evening class, but you'd need someone to watch your son. Don't assume it's impossible. Ask for help.

On Day One, you don't know when you'll need help from others, but you *will.* You'll need your people to be there to celebrate your successes and help when your system breaks. They'll make the journey less lonely and may even be the reason you reach the finish line.

In my family, we build support into our lives intentionally. Every New Year, we share one goal for each category: social, personal, professional, and stretch goals. My stretch goal last year was the plank world record. My son Kole's was about hockey. My mom usually focuses on volunteer work. We check in throughout the year to encourage each other, troubleshoot any barriers, and celebrate wins.

This is the best part about building your Day One team: Your goals could never be selfish because they're about more than just you. When your family and friends are part of the process, they benefit, too. Your hard work inspires them. It shows them that chasing big dreams is worth the discomfort and sacrifice. Your example gives them permission to go after their own goals.

Bringing people along for the journey helps you tailor your system to your needs. You can find accountability in others working toward similar goals, or get an outside perspective when you get stuck. A strong team gives you the confidence to experiment, learn from mistakes, and land on the path that works best for you.

Recognize Your Hard Stops

We've established that the best way to approach Day One of your goal is with a good support system *and* an experimental mindset. Let people cheer you on and show up to help, but remember: Outside voices can sometimes nudge you off course. That's why it's important to keep checking in with yourself. Growth will always feel uncomfortable, but if something only drains you or pulls you further from your goal, it may be time to adjust.

I learned that lesson when I tried kickboxing. I was already working out consistently, but I wanted a new challenge. I found a Groupon deal for kickboxing at a martial arts studio and decided to give it a try.

Immediately, I was hooked. Between the energy of the classes, the intensity of the workout, and the release of hitting a bag, it was exactly what I needed. Just like that, I had more information to support my goals, and I added kickboxing to my weekly routine.

Before long, the gym owner asked if I was up for an exchange: I'd teach kickboxing, and he'd train me to get my black belt in karate for free. I figured this could be another unexpected challenge to add to my training system, so I said yes.

But as it turned out, I hated karate.

It wasn't like kickboxing at all. Instead of a fun, high-energy workout, it felt like memorizing choreography. I admired the discipline it took to earn belts, but after a few weeks, I realized I was dreading the lessons.

So I had an uncomfortable choice to make: *Should I stick it out because I committed to the exchange? Or should I be honest and risk appearing unappreciative?*

In the end, I walked away from karate. Forcing myself to continue would have drained my motivation and risked creating a negative association with the gym altogether.

Discomfort is normal. It shows up anytime you push yourself. But when an activity consistently drains you with no positive return, that might be a hard stop.

When you hit resistance, ask yourself:

- Is this discomfort I can adapt to with time, or is it the wrong fit for me?
- Does this challenge energize me once I get going, or does it leave me dreading the next session?
- Will sticking with this help me move closer to my bigger goal, or further away?

If it's just discomfort, lean in and give your system time to adjust. If it's a hard stop, release it and move on. Quitting in this case isn't a failure. It means you had the courage to protect your bigger goal.

Cut out the habit of punishing yourself when you need to adjust, or when others' suggestions don't work out. Use hard stops as information to refine your path, or they'll become barriers between you and your goal.

Embracing Your New Identity

Day One is about who you're becoming. Even the first imperfect actions help you step into your new identity. Letting yourself own that identity and let go of the ones that don't align with your goal is a powerful act of self-support.

If running is your goal, start calling yourself a runner. If public speaking is your goal, start calling yourself a speaker. If painting is your goal, go ahead and call yourself an artist. The labels we give ourselves might not seem like a big deal, but they're important. They're a way of claiming what matters to us and reminding ourselves that we're learning to show up for what we want.

When I introduce myself, I feel confident saying, "I'm Rashelle Mason. I'm a mom, a wife, and an athlete." That doesn't mean I play sports professionally. It means athleticism is something I value and practice daily.

Be just as intentional about what you *don't* call yourself. Don't say, "I'm a smoker" if you're trying to quit. Say, "I'm quitting." Don't label yourself "lazy" if you're working on discipline. Say, "I'm building consistency." Replace the patterns you're leaving behind with language focused on where you're headed. Even if it feels awkward at first, presenting yourself with your new identity helps you embrace it.

Think about it like this: We wear t-shirts that announce something about us all the time. Look in my closet and you'll see fitness shirts that tell the world I train, a Punta Cana sweatshirt that says I love to travel, a "Warrior Mom" shirt from my kids' sports team, and even the Amazon vest from my delivery driver days. One of my favorites is a Guinness World Record shirt a friend gifted me to celebrate my plank journey.

You could see them as "just clothes," the same way you might dismiss how you introduce yourself as "just words." But your words are how you wear your identity. Don't wait until you've earned the new identity. Try it on now. Start on Day One.

Day One, Not One Day

Every frequent traveler knows the first few trips are the most chaotic. You overpack. You print papers you don't need. You stand in the wrong security line. But the more you travel, the more efficient you get. You figure out what actually matters, let go of what doesn't, and find your own rhythm.

That's what Day One is about. You've packed your bags with the tools and support you think you'll need. Now you're ready to start trying, learning, and refining. There will be wrong turns along the way, but each one helps you create a system flexible enough to adapt. You learn to roll with the uncontrollables and find what you *can* control to keep moving toward what you want.

So don't ask yourself if you're ready to achieve your entire goal today. Don't pressure yourself to have the whole journey mapped out. Instead, ask:

- Do I know my next step?
- Do I have what I need to start tomorrow?
- Am I willing to adapt when things don't go to plan?

If the answer is yes, you're ready to make the shift from "one day I will" to "I'm starting today." You're ready for Day One.

Chapter 8

STAYING MOTIVATED

Some days you won't feel like it.
Those are the days that count the most.
Keep going anyway. Show up. Do the work.
Each step forward proves you're stronger than your excuses.

—

"**B**ut Mom, I don't want to go on a hike. Why are you making us do this?"

That was the chorus from the backseat almost every time I suggested a family hike when my kids were younger. My daughter, Tyler, was always up for it, but my boys, Kyle and Kole, acted like walking in nature was a form of punishment.

So one day, I changed my approach.

Instead of hiking, I asked if they wanted to go geocaching. If you're not familiar, it's like a treasure hunt using GPS coordinates to find hidden containers filled with toys or trinkets. You can take an item from the container and leave something of equal value for the next person to discover.

With this reframe, my sons went from complaining and dragging their feet to running ahead of me. Suddenly, I couldn't keep up. They wanted to go geocaching all the time.

Now that Kyle is 23, he still doesn't really want to "hike" with me. But if there's a chance he might find a shed antler from a deer or elk, he's all in. Shed hunting is his new treasure hunting. We get to enjoy being outdoors together, but what makes us excited about it is still totally different.

That's how I want you to think about your big goal.

There comes a time during any major pursuit where the excitement fades. You'll get sick of it, and your friends and family may get sick of hearing you talk about it. That's normal.

You've made it past Day One, but you're still far from the finish line.

How you navigate the long stretch in the middle makes the difference between achieving your goal and giving up. This is when discipline and determination have to take over. It's where your mindset matters more than ever.

Like I did with my sons on our hikes, remind yourself that you can either see this pursuit as a punishment or an adventure. The work in front of you is the same either way. But how you *frame* it determines what you get out of the process, or whether or not you complete what you started.

That's why the days when you're over it are the most important ones to show up for.

So, when you start wondering why you signed up for this in the first place—and trust me, you will—let's make sure you know how to keep yourself on track.

The Adventure Reframe

Chasing a big goal often means working harder than you ever have before. So it's easy to slip into punishment mode without realizing it. The excitement can turn into pressure, and you may start to see the goal as restricting your life rather than helping you grow.

This is a natural pattern, but also an important one to recognize and disrupt. Because once your goal starts to feel like a punishment, negativity and resentment creep in—both of which only make it harder to stay consistent.

That's why I suggest the adventure reframe. Instead of seeing obstacles as proof that you can't succeed, recognize them as just part of the bigger adventure you're on. That way, you can let go of being mad at yourself, and instead get curious about ways to course-correct. Let's look at some examples.

Take the goal of saving money.

If you frame it as a punishment, it sounds like: *No more dinners out. No trips. No fun with the family until I reach this number.* You start to associate saving money with deprivation. Your goal should empower you, but this line of thinking turns it into a chore.

Now, frame saving as an adventure, and it sounds more like: *I'm learning and growing, even when I falter. I'm building a future of freedom and ease for my family. Look at all the fun things we can still do while saving—who knew?* Suddenly, the same goal becomes exciting, and you become more motivated to stick with it.

The same thing can happen with fitness goals. Someone who wants to lose weight might think: *I have to give up everything I love. I can't mess up, or I'll fail. Every imperfect day is proof that I can't do this.* But if you can see it as an adventure, the mindset becomes: *I'm learning to take care of my body. I'm testing my strength. Look how much I'm capable of. This can actually be fun.*

Which inner voice sounds more motivating, the punisher or the adventurer? Are you more likely to get up in the morning for a punishment or for an adventure? Which of the two will you be excited to stick with in the long run? For me, the adventurer wins every time.

If you find yourself losing motivation, try this reframe with the goal of making the journey more fun. You set this goal to challenge yourself, but that doesn't mean you can't enjoy the ride, too.

Once you've embraced the adventure mindset, the next step is learning how to make it enjoyable day to day.

Finding the Fun

When you hit an unexpected traffic jam on a road trip, you don't call yourself a failure or decide you'll never get to your destination. You reroute. You can still make it to where you're trying to go and enjoy a fun trip full of memories. The path may just look different from what you originally planned.

The same goes for your big goal. When things are harder or slower than expected, or you feel like you're losing steam, it doesn't mean you're off track. You may just need to change up your approach. You have to find the fun.

Maybe you build in little accomplishments along the way. You could celebrate at specific milestones rather than waiting for the "big day." Give yourself micro-victories to look forward to, and unique rewards for achieving them.

During plank training, I rewarded myself with an energy drink that I didn't have at any other time. I normally don't allow myself that much caffeine, but this beverage had electrolytes that helped with cramping, and I liked how it tasted, so it became a fun reward for plank days. It gave me something else to look forward to besides another day of hard work.

Think about parents who let their kids have soda on vacation when it's not allowed at home. That's not really about the drink itself. It's about making that specific context special so everyone has fun. Apply this idea to your goal. The daily work should never be a punishment. You can make everyday progress feel special just by creating small rituals around it.

The rituals don't have to be about giving yourself a treat, either. You can gamify the process, just like I did by turning hikes with my boys into a treasure hunt. What treasure can you collect? What small wins can you celebrate along the way?

Maybe you listen to a new playlist during long workouts, create a visual tracker and color in your progress, or plan a fun activity to celebrate specific phases of the journey. Finding the fun helps curb the feeling of "Are we there yet?" Instead, you enjoy the journey rather than white-knuckling the entire way to the destination.

The Opportunity Reframe

Even when you find the rituals and celebrations that make your path more enjoyable, there will still be days when it doesn't feel fun. So what do you do when you're just plain tired, frustrated, and ready to throw in the towel?

That's when it's important to find perspective, and nothing helps me press on quite like gratitude. But here's the trick I've discovered: Gratitude shouldn't be another item on your to-do list. It should be a reflection you practice often throughout the day.

A lot of people start the day by listing three things they're grateful for, but I've never been able to do that. I don't want gratitude to be just another task. So instead, I try to shift my thinking in the moments when I feel unmotivated. Rather than getting stuck in negativity, I draw on past experiences that reshaped how I see challenge and possibility.

When I was a nurse, I worked in a transitional care unit. Most of my patients were adults who'd experienced a sudden life-changing injury or illness. They went from living completely normal lives to navigating a tough diagnosis like multiple sclerosis or recovery after a tragic accident. Their stories impacted me deeply, but one young man in particular completely changed the way I think about opportunity.

He was just a normal eighteen-year-old when a major car accident left him unable to walk, sit up, or take care of even the smallest daily task. When he arrived, he had tubes and medical equipment supporting nearly every function of his body. For a long time, his journey wasn't even about making progress, just surviving another day.

But over time, I watched him choose to face not only discomfort, but also fight through unbearable pain and frustration every day for months. He relearned how to sit up and feed himself. Then he started standing with assistance. And eventually, against all odds, he was able to walk independently out of the facility and back to his life.

That level of determination and perseverance is rare for most of us to see firsthand. His story will forever stand out in my mind as an example of what's possible when someone refuses to quit.

Something about witnessing another person's push through the unthinkable reminded me that sheer human grit and willpower live in all of us. Watching him rebuild his life step by step reframed my own moments of resistance. It showed me that even in the hardest situations, we still have the choice to get up, try again, and make today mean something more than our current reality. We can see the work in front of us as an opportunity to make even one inch of progress toward the life we want.

This reframe of seeing today as an opportunity helped me get through plank training. When it felt exhausting, I told myself, *I don't have to do this. I get to do this.*

So if negativity starts to get the best of you when working toward your big goal, see if this reframe helps: Pursuing your goal isn't an obligation, but an opportunity.

Gratitude is like a muscle. It gets stronger the more you train it. So give yourself some grace as you work on this perspective shift. You won't always feel grateful for the "opportunity" to do something uncomfortable. But over time, this practice will help you appreciate how far you've come rather than dreading how far you have left to go.

Your Measures of Progress

In previous chapters, we talked about your "bag of proof," filled with the examples you've collected over time that prove you can get through hardship and accomplish challenging goals. But don't just rely on past experiences. Every inch of progress on this journey is proof that can sustain you when motivation fades.

This is why you need to have multiple ways of measuring your progress. For example, if you're trying to prioritize fitness, don't let the number on the scale be the only indicator of success. There are so many reasons that number can fluctuate, and without other ways to measure your effort, it's easy to get discouraged.

Don't forget all the other great things you're doing to move toward your goal. Tell yourself *I ate well today. I stayed hydrated. I treated myself better than I have in the past. I felt better after running than I used to.*

This can be as simple as acknowledging your daily habits:

- Did I show up today?
- How much time did I put in?
- Which skills have I improved?
- How do I feel now versus when I started?

The key is choosing measures of success that celebrate progress, not perfection.

During plank training, I didn't use fancy tracking tools. My measures were simple: how long I held a plank, how steady my breathing was, how I felt afterward, and how I handled unexpected pain. Another boost came from the people at the gym who told me I inspired them. Those regular reminders that I was making an impact on others became meaningful markers of progress. They were signs that I was still showing up for this goal.

Other times, the measurement was purely internal. I'd finish a hard session and realize I'd pushed through fatigue or self-doubt that might've stopped me before. It's important to make sure those mental milestones count, too.

You can reflect on these mentally, write them in your notebook or phone, or even log progress with photos. Anything that helps you see how far you've come is a powerful motivator to keep going.

When you measure progress, only two questions truly matter:

1. Did I do it?
2. Is it helping me get to my goal?

And remember, if the answer to that second question is no, you haven't failed. You've collected useful information. Use it to adjust and keep going.

Progress isn't always linear, and it can't always be measured in the ways you expect. But as long as you're still showing up, it's still happening. So find new forms of proof that the work you're putting in matters. Sometimes, that reminder is all you need to reignite motivation.

The Boredom Reframe

If you've been consistent for a while, there will come a point where you're not necessarily struggling. You're just bored. You're doing all the right things, staying disciplined, showing up day after day, and suddenly, the spark is gone.

The reframe here is simple: Boredom is good. It means you've grown. This isn't hard for you anymore. What was once uncomfortable is now routine—mundane even. You're ready for a new challenge.

Boredom is just your mind telling you it needs more. It's hungry. So if you feel bored, go ahead and celebrate that. Recognize that it isn't a reason to quit, but an indicator that it's time to move to the next level.

For example, maybe your goal in the past was to travel more. Traveling alone felt daunting, but then you got a job that required frequent work trips. Now, you travel all the time. Not only has it gotten easy, but you've almost gotten sick of traveling. So how do you make it fun again? Maybe during your next business trip, you call a friend to have dinner, go on a hike, or add in a day trip to a nearby town. Novelty is often the antidote to stagnation.

When it comes to your goal, this can be as simple as:

- trying a new class or teacher,
- listening to a new podcast while you train,
- reading a new book on a topic related to your goal, or
- buying new shoes or equipment to make practice feel fresh.

In the yoga world, we joke that "stealing" another instructor's move is actually a compliment. It means you were inspired. I'll often go to someone else's class so I can learn new poses or be reminded of ones I haven't done in a while. I leave feeling recharged and excited to bring that inspiration back to my own classes.

If things start feeling stale, apply this idea to your goal. Learn something new about the topic you're focused on. Pick up a complimentary skill that can strengthen your practice. Small changes can help reignite your passion for this pursuit.

You Don't Need Motivation

If you've reached the long stretch between Day One and the finish line, here's a secret you should know: You don't need motivation anymore. It's what got you started. It helped you show up for Day One. But motivation isn't reliable. It depends on positive emotions and best-case scenarios. So on the hard days when everything imaginable goes wrong, motivation may not show up at all.

If you want to stay in this, the two ingredients you need are discipline and joy.

Discipline is what gets you to do the work when you don't feel like it. It keeps you pushing through pain and negativity. Discipline doesn't bow out when you get knocked down. It asks you to get back up again.

Joy is what reminds you that this effort is worthwhile. It helps you find the fun and listen to your inner adventurer, rather than the punisher. Joy is what allows your goal to become meaningful, impact others, and transform challenge into growth.

Be relentless with both, because this long middle phase will test your discipline and your joy. Some days, you'll feel like you have nothing left to give. Your progress will feel invisible. Giving up will sound like the easiest "yes" of your life.

But you made it this far. You've already found discipline and joy in this goal, or you wouldn't be here. So don't wait for motivation to return. It might not.

Instead, focus on the facts:

- You've already come farther than you think.
- The hardest parts are where you grow the most.
- Growth doesn't always feel like progress in real time.

In the end, the bumps in the road often make for the best stories anyway. The hardest challenges come with the most powerful lessons. And the days you put in the work when you didn't feel like it shape your new identity.

This is the discomfort. You're in it now. Keep going. Let it change you.

Trust your discipline, keep your joy alive, and you'll make it to the end.

PART 3

THE BIG DAY AND BEYOND

Chapter 9
YOU'VE ARRIVED

You showed up when nobody cared.
You put in work no one saw.
Some days, you were your own worst critic;
Others, you were your own best coach and supporter.
You're still you, but look how you've grown.
No matter what's next, you made it.
You're here. You arrived.

—

At the crack of dawn on April 16, 2012, I laced up my running shoes for the Boston Marathon. Streetlights lit my walk to Boston Common as I checked my watch to make sure I'd catch the buses on time. I walked among other runners, and we exchanged smiles, knowing we were each feeling a similar mix of excitement and nerves.

After checking in, I boarded my bus and settled in for the hour-and-a-half ride to the starting line. I quickly realized I had two options: keep to myself and let my mind spiral, or talk to the other runners.

It would've been easy to see them as my competition, or a distraction stealing my focus on this big day. But this was my second marathon. I was confident I'd done everything I could to prepare. I knew my biggest threat at this stage was my own racing thoughts.

So I got to know the runner next to me. We laughed and swapped stories through the whole bus ride, then ended up waiting together in an open field until our waves were called. It was hours of sitting, stretching, and chatting, from dawn until my start time around 11:00 a.m., and connecting with the people around me made the time lighter.

And then, boom. A voice crackled over the loudspeaker.

Just like that, it was time to go.

On a big day like this, there's so much "hurry up and wait." You may have hours to sit in your own thoughts before doing one of the hardest things you've ever prepared for. I could've let the nerves build, glancing at my watch again and again until my start time. But I knew that would be agonizing, so I chose to find some fun in the waiting. I let people in.

Every goal has a version of this moment. In the weeks, months, or years of hard work you've put in, you've gathered tools to help you navigate the day when your goal finally becomes real. You're ready to show up and claim your new life, but how you approach this big moment is important too.

Preparing your mind, remembering how far you've come, and having fun along the way can make all the difference in how your journey progresses from here. So let's talk about how to best set yourself up for the day your goal is realized.

A Note About *Your* "Big Day"

In this chapter, I'll refer to the "big day" for goals that lead to one defining event, like running a marathon or giving a keynote speech. But your goal may be one you aim to sustain for a lifetime, like weight loss, a new role, or a long-term habit. The concepts that follow apply whether you're living out one significant moment or stepping into a new version of your life.

If your goal is about long-term lifestyle change, your "big day" begins the moment you realize you've built what you were working toward. From there, it's about owning it and showing up for yourself again and again. And even if your goal doesn't come with a final event, you can still choose a symbolic way to celebrate: putting on that outfit you once dreamed of wearing, hosting a celebration, or taking a quiet moment of reflection to honor how far you've come.

However, the culmination of your hard work looks, remember that reaching your goal marks both an arrival and a beginning. It's proof that you did the hard thing, and it's an invitation to keep showing up to own this new version of yourself.

The nerves will come no matter what. Just remember that discomfort is how you know you're growing. Parts of your big day may be brutal; others will be incredible. And it'll all be over in the blink of an eye. Before you know it, you'll wake up to the first morning of your new life.

As you step into this big moment, whether it's crossing a finish line or stepping into your new reality, trust yourself and the preparation that brought you here. There's nothing else you need to do. You're ready.

So let yourself be present for what comes next. The excitement and the nerves, the people around you who've fought their own battles to get here, the buzzing energy in the air—it's all part of the experience you've worked hard to earn.

Take it in and enjoy. This is the fun part. It's time to party.

Make It a Party

When Mike Tyson returned to the ring at 58 years old, I admired his philosophy around training versus the big day. His opponent was Jake Paul, a heavyweight boxer in his twenties, and the two of them approached preparation very differently.

Jake was showy when news outlets filmed him training. He wore bling, blasted loud music, and talked a big game. But when Mike Tyson interviewed, he spoke about his training as work, and the big day as "the party."

The way he saw it, the fight was like a celebration of the process that got him here. That's when you turn up the lights, play the music, wear the bling, and enjoy what you've earned.

I tend to approach my big days the same way. The day I attempted to beat the planking world record, the local Channel 12 news crew showed up at the gym. I didn't know they were coming, but here they were, requesting an interview ten minutes before my countdown clock was set to begin.

Everyone around me panicked. "Tell them no! You need to get in the zone!"

But I figured, what else was I going to do for ten minutes? I was ready. So I said yes.

The interview was one of the best decisions I made that day. It kept me in a light, playful mindset leading up to the challenge, and the crew ended up staying for the entire five-hour event, which added to the atmosphere. The same newscaster I watched on TV every day, who didn't know me from Adam, stood right next to my family, cheering, "You've got this, Rashelle! You can do it!"

That's the fun energy I hope you find at this point in your journey. Whether your goal comes with a "big day" or it's the new life you maintain day after day, don't stay trapped inside your own head. Smile. Breathe. Engage. Let yourself have fun with it.

This party approach doesn't diminish your effort. I actually see it as the best way to honor it. When you take your goal too seriously, you communicate a few unhelpful *and* untrue messages to yourself:

1. I don't trust that I put in enough effort to satisfy my "why."
2. My performance matters more than the hard work that led me here.
3. I can control the uncontrollable variables that come up if I just think harder.

That's not the headspace you want to be in leading up to something so important.

So believe in yourself. Celebrate the process. Recognize that there will always be aspects outside of your control. Now that the moment is here, the best way you can support yourself is to find the fun in it. The more you allow yourself to enjoy the experience, the calmer and more grounded you'll feel when it counts.

Make It Familiar

I know finding the fun might sound easier said than done. Big moments can come with butterflies, or even the kind of anxiety that ties your stomach up in knots. So how do you get into a state of mind where enjoying the experience is even possible?

You make it familiar.

I tried to make my plank day as much like a training day as possible. I wore the same clothes I trained in. I used the same mat. I queued up the same music and motivational speeches that got me through months of planking on my own.

The fewer new variables you introduce, the less you give your mind to worry about. Stick with what's worked up to now—the processes your mind and body have already formed habits around:

- Wake up at the same time.
- Keep the same routines.
- Eat and drink the same things.
- Wear the same clothes.
- Use the same gear.

For example, don't buy a new pair of heels for a big work presentation. They may pinch in a way you didn't expect, and suddenly your mind will focus on the pain instead of the moment. Don't drink coffee or even take a new supplement if it's not an established part of your day. You have enough going on. This isn't the time to experiment, no matter how small it seems.

And for long-term goals or lifestyle changes, these patterns are just as important. Stick with the habits that got you this far, and be intentional when introducing new elements into the equation. Because when your brain recognizes a familiar rhythm, it stops scanning for danger. That frees up energy to focus on the task at hand.

So with a big event, if you didn't do it when preparing, don't do it now. One of the tools you can leverage in advance is the way you visualize the moment, as we discussed in chapter 6. Here's where this tool really comes in handy. You can make the experience of living out your goal more familiar by visualizing, rehearsing, or role-playing how it will go before it happens.

In my cross-country days, I walked the course before a race so I could picture where I'd need to push the hardest. Before my marathons, I ran the full 26.2 miles in training. I didn't stop at 23, even though many runners say that's far enough. For me, confidence came from knowing I'd already done it.

The same was true for planking. My goal was to last five hours, so I planked for five hours eight times leading up to the event. By the end of my training, I was planking for five hours twice a week. I know that sounds extreme, but I felt a *need* to do it frequently enough to remind myself that I could still do it. If too many days passed, I started thinking, *five hours? How did you do five hours?* I couldn't even explain to myself how I could get my body to do it.

That repetition allowed the big day to feel as familiar as possible. That's why I felt calm enough to take that last-minute news interview. I didn't need to overthink it. I already had proof in the bag that I could do this.

You can build familiarity in simpler ways, too. Some marathon runners go for a jog before the race starts, even though they have 26.2 miles ahead of them. A friend of mine who competes in Ironmans, triathlon races that start with a 2.4-mile open-water swim, gets in the water beforehand to prepare her body.

It may seem counterproductive, but taking familiar steps ahead of your big moment isn't a waste of energy. It helps avoid a shock to your system. You don't want to go from zero to ten. If you can, find ways to go from *five* to ten instead.

This works in professional settings too. Before my first national meeting after being promoted to vice president of sales, I practiced my opening presentation over and over. I shut my office door, walked through the slides as if I were presenting to my new team, timed myself, and refined the delivery until it felt natural. By the time I got to my presentation day, I could've given it in my sleep.

The thing is, you never master something that's really hard. It's always going to be hard. But the more you practice, the more confidence you have when approaching a big day or living out a new habit. That way, when the nerves hit, you can take a breath and think to yourself, *this is going to suck, but I can do it.*

Clear the Junk

One of my go-to sayings while working toward a big goal is "embrace the suck." Don't shy away from it. Don't expect it to be easy. When you accept that discomfort will be with you at every step, it loses some of its power.

That said, you don't need *extra* junk weighing you down. The hardest part of reaching your goal should be the challenge itself, not inner turmoil or outside negativity. So if it doesn't help you stay grounded or achieve your goal, it has to go. That means clearing as much internal and external clutter as possible. Here's how I recommend doing that, whether you're approaching a "big day" or setting yourself up for long-term change:

1. Anticipate uncontrollables

Expect something to go wrong, or at least differently than you thought, because it will. When you expect perfection, your mindset crumbles when things get messy. But when you've primed your mind for the unexpected, you're better able to handle it when it comes.

The day of my Boston Marathon, it was ninety-five degrees outside. A ninety-five degree day in April, in Boston. Of course, no one could have anticipated that. Race officials even offered us the chance to defer to the next year because of the extreme heat. But I'd trained too long to back out.

That day was miserable. My outfit, which I'd picked carefully to prevent chafing, didn't work in the heat. I cramped up. I couldn't walk normally for three days afterward. My time was almost double the marathon I'd run two years prior. But I finished.

While I couldn't have prepared for that kind of heat, I'm grateful that I went in expecting unforeseen obstacles and chose to run anyway. Not just to prove something to myself, but because if I'd deferred, the 2013 race I would've run was when the tragic Boston Marathon bombings took place.

It's another example—an extreme one—of how you can do everything right and still face unimaginable circumstances. I've learned that lesson more than once.

When training for the planking goal, my left arm never went completely numb during any of the eight times I planked for five hours, but it did on my attempt day. With two hours remaining on the clock, I had to accept that I'd have to fight without that arm. But again, I had prepared for the unexpected.

While I couldn't plan for these exact things to go wrong, I did plan for *something* to go wrong. So I was mentally prepared to pivot when it did. That's what you're doing here: priming your mind to expect challenges so you're not thrown by them. You simply adjust, breathe, and press on.

2. Shine a light on the worst thing

When my son, Kole, gets nervous before a hockey game, I ask him, "What's the worst that can happen?" Instead of spiraling through every possibility, I encourage him to go straight to the one worst possible outcome, just for a moment.

"It's not going to happen, but let's just say it does. What then?"

Often, the answer is simple. It might hurt. I might wish things had gone differently. But I can get through this.

If you take a moment to get specific about the thing you fear most and make peace with it, its grip on your mind will ease. It might even start to seem silly. Playing out that worst-case scenario is like finally facing the monster under the bed. When you stop hiding and shine a light on the scary thing, you realize it was never a beast lurking in the shadows. It was just a pile of old clothes.

I did this in my early fitness coaching days too. When I felt uncomfortable teaching my first classes, I asked myself: *What if I just ran out of here? How will I feel afterward? Relieved or disappointed?* I knew the answer right away. I'd feel awful, because walking away would mean letting fear win over something I really wanted.

Okay, I'll stick it out. But what if I screw up? Well then, I screw up. People screw up all the time. You're a human teaching a room full of humans. They'll understand.

Once I pictured the absolute worst outcomes, I realized they weren't as terrifying as they felt in my head. The unknown is always scarier than the truth.

So don't approach your goal with that worst-case scenario still creeping in the shadows. Shine a light on it. Get to know that fear well so it doesn't control your path ahead.

3. Remove what drains you

Now, let's look at the external. If there's negativity around you leading up to your big moment, do what you can to get away from it. You've spent months, maybe years, preparing for this. You don't need anyone or anything chipping away at your confidence right now.

Whether it's a person, external drama, or your own negative thoughts, be selfish with what gets your focus today. This is your time.

It's much harder to achieve something big while your internal and external worlds pull you down with negativity. If you believe things will go wrong, they probably will. If you expect to fail, your body and mind will start to operate as if failure is inevitable.

When my son misses a shot in hockey, he might say, "I suck." I always tell him, "Well, you do now, because that's what you're telling yourself. You don't suck. You had one bad hit. Big difference."

Everything from the people you surround yourself with to the words you say and the thoughts you think affects your reality. Your day will go better if you fill it with "I've got this" rather than "I can't."

So remove as much negativity as possible and focus on what fuels you instead. If it helps, replace negative thoughts with positive mantras. Here are a few I kept in mind on my plank day:

- You are fine.

- Embrace the suck.
- You're not going to die.
- The pain is temporary.

4. Make time to clear your mind

Even with all of the preparation in the world, your mind will still look for things to worry about. That's normal. The goal isn't to eliminate your nerves, just to quiet them.

So another way to help yourself enjoy the experience of living out your goal is to give yourself plenty of time—more than you think you need—to meditate, visualize, breathe, and get your mind right.

This is important because your mind doesn't fully distinguish between imagining something and actually doing it. That's why your hands get clammy and your heart races when imagining something scary, like peering over a cliff's edge. You can use that mental wiring to your advantage.

For me, that quiet time often comes in the morning. Before the chaos of a big day starts, I visualize what's ahead. I picture myself prepared and fully present. For you, that might look like journaling, meditation, prayer, or shaking out the nerves to your favorite music.

5. Open your bag of proof

Finally, go back to your past successes. Think about the challenges you've overcome. They don't need to have anything to do with the goal ahead of you. The point is that you've done hard things before. And regardless of the outcome, you made it out on the other side.

When your nerves start to rise, pull out that mental bag of proof. Remember all the hard work you put in. The pain you pushed through. The late nights and early mornings. The times when life knocked you down and you got back up. Let those memories fill the air around you. In moments of doubt, they can remind you that you have what it takes.

Feed Off the Energy

When you make time to clear your mind, it's easier to be present with the energy around you when it's time to "party." Just like I did with the news crew on plank day and with the other runners before the Boston Marathon, letting people in gives you more fuel for the journey ahead.

During the days leading up to my world record attempt, a local radio host I'd chatted with during training asked if he could call me on the big day. I joked, "Why not? I'll have nothing else to do!" And sure enough, about an hour into my plank, the phone rang. I answered, live on the radio.

Everyone thought I was out of my mind. "You're in the middle of a world record attempt! Why are you talking on the phone?"

But it didn't take any energy; it was a nice distraction. The whole radio team cheered and kept me smiling. Finding moments to share the experience gave me energy and made the whole day more fun.

When you stay in your own bubble, it's easy to assume people are judging you. But most of the time, they're rooting for you. So on your big day, don't turn inward. Broaden your support team. If you're in a race, don't look at your competition as villains in your story. Wish them luck. If you're giving a presentation, compliment the other speakers. Tell them you loved what they had to say. And if you're making a long-term lifestyle change, invite supportive people into your corner for the long haul.

Since my plank day, I've had people come up and say, "Oh, you're the planker!" They'd watched the livestream or seen the news segment. So even though I've never met them, we had this connection because I chose to let people in.

It's the same reason we love sports. We don't know the players, but we still celebrate and feel part of the experience. Even elite athletes like Simone Biles show the power of letting others in. When she opened up about her mental health struggles, people rallied behind her. Many saw themselves in her story and felt less alone because of it.

Give yourself permission to let people in on your goal. Don't tune out the cheers. Let them hype you up. Feed off that energy and let it remind you: No matter how individual your goal might seem, you're never really doing it alone.

Maybe your finish line is every day you choose to maintain what you've built—every meal, every workout, or every calm response instead of an old habit. The celebration looks different, but the mindset is the same: trust your preparation, stay present, and honor the work it takes to keep showing up.

Fight to the Finish

This is it. The moment you've worked so hard for. You've prepared your mind, cleared the junk, built your confidence, and surrounded yourself with the right energy.

Trust the work that led you here. It's time to carry yourself into that party like you belong there, because you do.

Stand tall. Chest up. Chin up. Smile.

Let your body take up space.

Take slow, deep breaths.

You've been here before in one way or another. All the practice, every other challenge you've faced, has brought you to this moment. You've already grown. You've already won. Nothing can take that from you.

Your next step isn't about proving anything to anyone. You're showing up fully for a moment you've earned.

All that's left to do is to ask yourself: *What do I want to happen, and how hard am I willing to push myself to get it?*

What will it feel like to empty your tank and celebrate what you've built?

This is your party. Give it everything you've got.

See you on the other side.

Chapter 10
WHAT'S NEXT

I hope you're proud
Of your strength when things got tough.
Your resilience when plans went sideways.
Your determination to stick it out 'til the end.
I hope you see beautiful lessons, not "what ifs."
I hope you feel gratitude, not regret.
I hope you look back on this adventure fondly.
And look forward to the magic yet to come.

—

I still had open wounds on my elbows from my plank world record attempt when people started asking, "So, what's next?" It felt like they wanted to hear me say I had my sights set on a record for push-ups, or something even bigger.

After reaching a big goal, it's easy to get swept up in the opinions of others. But this is a crucial time to pause and explore what *you* want. Otherwise, "what's next" is a daunting question. Standing there, having just poured everything you had into something extraordinary, you may find yourself thinking, *Oh no…what is next?*

You might feel a little lost, like there's a void where your regimented training schedule or practice sessions used to be. That's normal. Even if your goal was about creating a long-term change, like eating healthier, getting better with money, or starting a new career, once you find your rhythm, you may start to crave a new challenge.

No matter how you feel on the other side of your goal, you have to decide what's next for *you*. If I'd let myself be convinced to chase another world record to impress others, my "why" wouldn't have been strong enough to get me there.

So it's okay if unexpected feelings come up in the days and weeks following your big accomplishment. Don't rush to fill the void. Give yourself time to reflect on what you've learned and how you've grown. Let yourself be proud of the mental toughness you've built and the skills you developed along the way. When you create space to debrief, you'll start to sense the nudges pointing toward your next right step.

The Final Assessment

Whether your goal involved a big, final event or lasting change, the part where you're pushing yourself is behind you now. The crowd has dispersed. Maybe you feel sore, exhausted, or vulnerable. There's no next step on the calendar, either because you're finished or because you've successfully integrated a long-term goal into your life.

Before you reach for the next thing, look back and ask yourself:

1. How did it go?
2. Did I fulfill my "why?"

In most cases, the path to a big goal doesn't unfold exactly as planned. Detours happen. Your "why" may have changed throughout the process. So when assessing your journey, you need to dig deeper than "win or lose."

Revisit Your "Why"

Before I ran my first marathon in 2010, I expected it to be my *only* marathon. My "why" was simple: I wanted to prove I could finish. Shan and I had just gotten married, and once the race was over, the next goal was to try for a baby.

But to my surprise, my race time meant I qualified for the Boston Marathon—a huge honor in the running world. Immediately, I knew I wouldn't be able to let this opportunity pass me by. *Oh great*, I chuckled to myself, *I guess we're running the Boston!*

The catch was that you had two years to run the Boston Marathon before you'd have to qualify again. And on top of that countdown, I had my biological clock to think about. I was thirty-nine, and we wanted a baby.

By some miracle, I managed both. I had Kole in July of 2011, almost exactly nine months after that first marathon. Of course, he was my priority, and I didn't want to do anything that would jeopardize either of our health. But after speaking with my doctors, I realized it was still possible to run in Boston without requalifying. So I picked up training again around my newborn-mom feeding and sleep schedule, and I was ready to race in April 2012.

Looking back, that season of life completely reframed my "why." This time, I didn't care about getting a faster time or impressing anyone. The deeper purpose was just honoring and enjoying the unexpected chance to be there. That perspective turned out to be a gift, because as I shared in chapter 9, my Boston Marathon didn't go the way I imagined.

I was expecting a crisp, fifty-degree spring morning. Instead, we got dangerous, unseasonable heat. When my finisher's plaque arrived with my final time printed across the bottom, almost double my first marathon time, I laughed. Not out of embarrassment, but because what looked like a "worse" race on paper was actually the one that proved my strength the most. Postpartum marathon training at forty. Running through heat that could've justified quitting. I'd exceeded my expectations with my first marathon, so my time in Boston might have deflated me in the past, but I knew to look deeper. A plaque could never capture the growth and confidence I gained from crossing that finish line.

My plank day taught me a similar lesson. Even having planked for five hours eight times before, I couldn't make it happen that day. Like the joke I sometimes make about my messy golf swing, I "came in ugly." I had to force my body to stay up with a numb arm, and instead of reaching five hours, I only managed nine seconds past the record time.

Would I have preferred a better outcome? Yes.

But my inner critic was happy because of *why* I did it. Not how it went.

And when I thought about it, I didn't want to be the person who made this goal look effortless, anyway. Maybe my struggle that day made me more relatable, or encouraged someone else to stick with something that feels impossibly hard. When I could look past that performance, my final assessment of the plank experience was almost better because of the struggle I had to overcome.

That's why it's so important to reflect after reaching a goal. The outcome of your hard work may not match the original plan. You're likely to be your own worst critic if things didn't turn out as you'd hoped. But it'd be a mistake to see an imperfect outcome as a failure. Revisit the "why" that goes deeper than a race time, a prize, a title, or the number on the scale.

Recognize all the growth and learning you did to get here. No matter what happened, you have a lot to be grateful for—so much to add to your bag of proof that you're someone who shows up for their goals. This reflection is where you unearth the real wins.

Who Are You Now?

The next questions to ask yourself are:

1. How do I feel?

2. What am I going to do with what I gained from this goal?

These questions both matter more than the surface-level "What's next?" But depending on your goal, the outside opinions might be loud after you achieve it. So carve out time to check in with yourself before moving ahead. You may feel things you didn't expect. You'll gain clarity you couldn't have had before you started this journey.

I didn't try to force my "what's next" after my plank challenge. I felt grateful, and I leaned into a nudge about what I wanted to *do* with the lessons I gained. The answer I gave wasn't the flashy soundbite interviewers may have hoped for, and that's okay. It was simple, but it was my truth: *I want to give back.*

I'm at a stage where I've felt the rush of working hard and reaching a big goal many times. Now I want to help others feel it too. It's why I've started private wellness coaching and speaking at events, and why I decided to write this book.

The nudge you feel after reaching your goal might be completely different. If your goal had an end date, like a race or fitness challenge, you might wake up the next day with that roller-coaster feeling: You were freaking out in the beginning, psyching yourself up to do something scary. But now that it's all over, you look around and say, "That was so much fun. Let's do it again!"

You might enjoy the challenge more the second time because there's less pressure. Or maybe you're drawn to repeat it because your "why" isn't fully satisfied yet. Whether the outcome wasn't what you expected or you still have something to prove to yourself, you feel that tug to start from Day One again.

You're not the same person who started this journey. So this is your chance to get to know the new you. Don't get in a hurry or lose yourself in the aftermath. Use what you've gained to find joy and direction beyond what you dreamed was possible.

Feeding the Discomfort Muscle

In the process of pursuing any big goal, you train your discomfort muscle. You expand your window of tolerance for uncertainty, awkwardness, and even fear.

This is worth celebrating. Because look at what you did:

You took fear and made it fun.

Don't retreat now. Keep growing. Find new ways to lean into discomfort. That feeling of pushing past your comfort zone may have been terrifying at first, but it can become energizing, even addictive. You've already proven you can do hard things. If you keep going, that discomfort muscle can help you achieve more than you ever dreamed.

But there's a difference between *feeding* that muscle and *forcing* it.

For some, growth from here might mean repeating the same challenge. If that's you, make sure you're doing it out of enjoyment rather than obligation. You hear about people who fall back in love with their passions once they're no longer doing them professionally. That's what I mean. If this goal still lights you up, keep at it. But if you feel pressure to outdo yourself, pause to make sure your head and your "why" are in the right place.

For example, even though I "came in ugly" on my plank world record attempt, I have no desire to repeat it. If I tried again, it would be for the wrong reasons: to impress others or massage my ego. Instead, what excites me now is being part of other people's triumph stories. Helping others pursue big goals gives meaning to my own hard work, struggles, and successes.

You get to choose how you keep stretching from here. "What's next?" doesn't have to match the intensity of your previous goal. It just has to keep you excited, growing, and engaging with life.

From "Me" to "We"

I've talked about the importance of letting people in on your goals from the beginning, and here's one reason why: A major pursuit can feel lonely, isolating, and even selfish. But it doesn't have to.

When you share your wins, setbacks, and lessons with others, your goal becomes bigger than you. It stops being just about your personal growth and turns into a chance to make a real impact.

If you're proud of how your goal went, sharing what you learned will multiply that joy. If you're not satisfied, helping others can get you out of your head and remind you that all your hard work matters. Even if you're still finding your own next step, you can give meaning to what you've achieved by helping someone else take theirs.

It's a natural evolution, just like athletes who become coaches, cancer survivors who volunteer, or mentors like Warren Buffett who see incredible success, then turn around to share what they've learned. Once you've climbed a mountain, the next instinct is to reach back and help someone else up.

Speaking and coaching others has brought my journey full circle. Helping others gives me deeper satisfaction from what I've achieved. And since public speaking still pushes me out of my comfort zone, these endeavors keep me growing too.

When I was invited to speak to a high school swim team, I was honored, but unsure what I could offer. I thought, *I'm a fifty-three-year-old woman walking into a room full of teenagers. What could I possibly say that would land?* But when I stood in front of them, the pressures of my high school cross country days came flooding back: the self-doubt, the comparisons, and the weight of other people's expectations.

One girl raised her hand and asked, "How do you deal with haters?"

That's when I realized how universal our struggles are. I may have been old enough to be the girl's mother, but we both faced similar issues. Even as an adult, I dealt with people on social media criticizing my world record attempt.

I told her that if someone spends their energy tearing you down, it's because you've captured their attention. Jealousy and judgment are just immature forms of recognition. You're doing something that forces them to confront their own excuses, and they don't like that. It's not about you, so don't waste your energy trying to change their minds. Just keep going.

What was supposed to be a twenty-minute talk turned into an hour-long conversation. That day showed me that no matter our age or background, we all share similar fears, and we can all learn from one another.

Around the same time, a local cross-country coach brought some of his runners to a free yoga class I teach in my backyard. They'd never done yoga before, but five high school boys showed up anyway, willing to try something new. A week later, the coach told me that three of them set personal records at their next race. Maybe yoga helped, maybe it didn't, but they *believed* it did, and they're excited to come back for more.

Playing a small role in those personal records felt as fulfilling as setting one myself. In using your experience to help others, you get to be part of their story and relive the excitement for yourself, too.

And if you feel lost or unsatisfied at the end of your journey, you'll still benefit from helping others. You don't have to wait until you feel gratitude or abundance to give back. In fact, giving to others often *creates* those feelings. The moment you give, you tell yourself that you have enough to share with others. That automatically puts you in a state of gratitude.

Gratitude, to me, is the highest level of wellness—the peak emotion we all strive for—because it's the expression of true happiness and contentment with your life. And nothing helps you find it faster than connection. When you step outside the bubble you've lived in while chasing your goal and rejoin the world around you, you gain a clearer view of what it all meant. With that clarity, you're more able to hear the quiet nudges pointing toward what's next for you.

Your Next Challenge

What was once a big, scary goal is now behind you, which means that it's time to prepare for a life beyond what you thought was possible. If that feels intimidating, good. That's how we know we're on the right path, remember?

You don't need a grand plan for what's to come. Some of the most amazing adventures in life happen because of a subtle nudge—a moment you decided to lean in and trust your intuition.

That's how I got started writing this book. A few important people in my life said I should tell my story. The first time I heard it was from Shan, and I thought, *Well, you're my husband. Of course you'd say that.*

Then I heard it again from my old boss, and again from people I didn't expect. Each time, it resonated a little more. So, just like when I felt pulled to try the Facebook plank challenge, I explored the nudge. And look where it led.

Some nudges are big and life-changing, but even the ones that feel silly can be important. Recently, my fourteen-year-old asked me to coach his hockey team's dry-land practices. My first thought was, *Why would a group of teenage boys want to take instruction from a fifty-three-year-old woman?*

The nudge was simple: Kole thinks it'd be cool for me to do this, and it's rare to be cool in front of him right now. That's all it took, and now I'm diving into a new challenge without a clue what I'm doing.

That's the best part, though. You don't need to know what you're doing. You've already proven that you can start from uncertainty, push through tough challenges, and find your way. You did that with your big goal, and that process led to incredible things.

So that's all you need to do now. Listen for the nudges, big and small. They may already be there. And now that space has cleared in your mind and your calendar, you're in the perfect place to hear them. Before you know it, you'll find yourself on Day One of something new. Stronger yet still uncomfortable. Wiser, yet still terrified. And that's how you'll know the time has come again, to *just start*.

CONCLUSION

It wasn't easy. In fact, it was brutal.
It pushed you to your limit. Stole the air from your lungs.
It demanded blood, sweat, tears—the hardest
fight of your life.
But look what it gave you: fulfillment beyond measure.
Proof of your grit, strength, and capacity for growth.
A wild, messy, beautiful journey that's forever yours.
All because you claimed a life unruled by fear.

—

When someone asks me, "What would you do differently next time?" my answer is simple: nothing. That's what it means to have an empty tank. You know you gave everything you had, even if the outcome isn't what you pictured.

That's how I felt as the confetti settled on the gym floor after my planking world record attempt. Satisfied that I'd risen to the challenge, given it my all, and fulfilled my "why" even though I "came in ugly," my arm went numb in hour three, and it was a battle to make it past the record of four hours, thirty minutes, and eleven seconds.

I walked away feeling like I'd already won, like my community and I had accomplished something amazing together. But that mindset was put to the test when I got the news.

As I sat in front of my computer, rereading the email from Guinness World Records for the tenth time, the words stared back at me in bold letters:

"We do not accept."

I did *not* break the world record for longest female elbow plank.

Yes, I held a plank longer than the record time. But upon reviewing footage from the day, Guinness determined that my form moved outside of their parameters more than once in those final thirty minutes.

Anyone's first response to news like this is the desire to run backwards. *Can we just rewind to a few minutes ago, before I read that email?* But part of me already knew. Even that day, as I fought to stay up with one numb arm, I was concerned about my form. I celebrated making it past the record time with the crowd who'd cheered me on, but I left the event wondering if the official result from Guinness might not go my way.

I sat with that email for a long time, thinking back to other moments in my life when something didn't turn out how I'd hoped.

Is this like my cross-country injury? My divorce? My job loss?

Could I have done something differently?

Did I fail? Did I give up too early?

Did I give in to comfort?

But before I could spiral, my mind went still. *The answer is NO.*

My inner critic wasn't getting the final word this time. Because the ultimate test of mental toughness isn't emerging victorious from every battle. It's having the courage to go all in on something, knowing you might empty your tank and *still* not get the result you fought for. It's choosing grace over self-criticism. It's recognizing the wins, even if they come in a different form than you imagined.

I made peace with the result, because my "why" was never about making it into a book of world records anyway.

My "why" was everything that challenge gave me during the year I trained: discipline, confidence in myself, and purpose as I navigated a tough season of life. But along the way, my "why" grew beyond my expectations. I saw my actions inspire others. My community came together to celebrate fitness and support one another. And through my plank event, we raised over $20,000 for veterans through the Catch A Lift Fund.

This journey not only gave me a sense of purpose when I needed it most; it gave me a new purpose in life. That's why you're reading this book.

So, did I fail? No. I grew beyond what I could imagine.

Owning Your Truth

Even after reckoning with my inner critic, I still worried about how people would react to the news that I hadn't beaten the world record after all. I could regain my confidence sitting at my computer alone, but the thought of telling others brought up shame and embarrassment. I dreaded seeing disappointment on their faces.

My inner critic would've had me hide so I didn't have to talk about the result. But I thought back to the times I've owned my truth, like when I let my tiny hometown in on the secret that I'd moved back home with a toddler, a baby on the way, and a divorce in progress. Fear is more painful than confronting the truth.

In fact, owning your truth gives you a level of freedom and power you can't access if you stay hidden. It feels like finally exhaling after holding your breath all day. So I gave people the chance to support me through this too. And they did.

The first person I told wasn't a family member or best friend. It was Larry Sorensen, host of the *Autumn Athletes* podcast. We had just finished recording an episode about my world record attempt, and I knew he planned to release it soon. I didn't want the episode to mislead anyone now that I had the official news.

I called him and said, "If you don't want to publish the interview, I get it."

But Larry didn't hesitate.

"Oh, no, no, no. We're doing this," he said. "You planked for over four hours. You still did something amazing. The fact that, due to technicalities, they didn't make it official…does that take away what you did? Of course not."

Hearing that from him meant a lot. We decided to re-record the interview to include the news from Guinness. By the end of that conversation, we were both in tears. Larry's an athlete too, and he understood what it means to pour yourself into something that doesn't go as planned.

But speaking the truth out loud helped me see that my planking journey gave me much more than I expected—so many valuable lessons to share with others. The process of owning my truth allowed me to own a sense of peace about the outcome too.

The Real Point of All of This

Sometimes the goal you set is just the vehicle that gets you moving. You think you're working toward a title or a finish line, but what you gain along the way ends up mattering far more than the outcome.

My goal of breaking the world record gave me purpose and something outside of my difficult circumstances to focus on. But ultimately, the record itself didn't matter.

If I had to choose between seeing my name in a record book or reliving this experience and everything it gave me, I'd forgo the title ten thousand times over. The purpose, growth, and community I found through this journey were the real wins.

Outcomes are uncontrollable anyway. All you can control is your next move. Will you beat yourself up, or will you let yourself savor the unexpected wins? Will you see this as a failure, or as proof that you were brave enough to try? Will you make disappointment your identity, or will you use it as fuel to keep growing?

Where You Go From Here

Here are the deeper truths behind any meaningful pursuit:

1. The only real way to avoid disappointment is to never try.
2. Discomfort is a price worth paying for a life fully lived.
3. The only real loss is to stop growing.

If there's one thing my planking journey taught me, it's that growth doesn't end at the finish line *unless you let it.* There's always another mountain waiting to be climbed, another version of yourself asking to be brought to life.

So whether you're currently celebrating a win, reflecting on a setback, or starting something new, I hope my story reminds you that it's worth taking that next small, uncomfortable step today. *Just start.* You'll never stop growing if you refuse to stop showing up.

To *staying* uncomfortable,

Rashelle Mason

Would personalized accountability help you reach your goal?

My one-on-one wellness coaching is designed to keep you moving forward, even through motivation dips and setbacks. Sound like it might help? Start by booking a free thirty-minute consultation. We'll chat about what you need to maintain strong habits and achieve long-term success.

Visit www.riseshineco.com for coaching and speaking inquiries.

ACKNOWLEDGEMENTS

To my family: my husband, Shan; my daughter, Tyler; and my sons, Kyle and Kole, thank you for being my constant. When someone pursues a big goal, their family makes sacrifices too, and that doesn't go unnoticed. You've supported me through every season of imbalance: When I was training six hours a day, tired, distracted, or gone too much. You've been there through everything, and I'm so grateful.

Shan, every time I come to you with another big idea, you say, "Really? All right, here we go!" Your patience and endless support mean the world to me.

To the entire Princeton Club family—members, staff, and leadership—thank you for believing in me. Had you not trusted me to pursue my world record attempt and the event surrounding it, I don't know if it would have happened. It certainly wouldn't have been the same without each and every one of you. I came to you with an audacious goal, and you didn't hesitate. You said yes. To CEO Andy Haugen, General Manager Renee Warzon, Manager Erin Faught, and the rest of the team, your encouragement made all the difference.

Thank you to Andy Smith, my neighbor, friend, and the veteran who kept me going on plank day. Your willingness to share your story gave me perspective when I needed it most and reminded me what "hard" truly means. And a special thank-you to Colin Gregory, Owner and Director of Photography at Sinclair Collective, who captured my journey on video and brought this story to life in a way I couldn't have imagined.

I'd also like to acknowledge myself for facing difficult circumstances and turning them into growth opportunities. Losing my job when the business closed, facing rejection when seeking new work, and experiencing mental health challenges were never part of the plan. But none of this would've happened without my ability to power through and find purpose despite it all. I'm grateful for this journey, exactly as it unfolded, and for where it's led: to a new chapter of helping others through wellness coaching.

And finally, thank you, the reader. If you've made it through this book, your inner voice is telling you to go after something big. Thank you for trusting that nudge. Your bravery will show others that it's worth following your intuition, even if you don't yet know where it will take you. We all deserve to know the beauty and purpose of a life beyond comfort. Thank you for setting that example.

RESOURCES

I n this book, we've talked about "packing your bags" with supportive tools to prepare for the hard work that comes with pursuing a big goal. What's in your bag will be unique to you. But as a starting point, I'm sharing a few resources that have helped me, plus some ways to get additional support on your journey.

Get Fired Up for Any Big Moment: *Motiversity*

Motiversity is a collection of motivational speeches by athletes, business leaders, and other inspiring figures. I play one every morning on my way to the gym to get my mindset right for the day.

Listen on Spotify,[3] YouTube,[4] and other streaming platforms by searching "Motiversity."

Learn from the Greats: *The School of Greatness by Lewis Howes*

Lewis Howes finds fascinating, high-profile guests to interview and asks great questions. You pick up nuggets of wisdom and practical tools you can use right away.

---

3 *Motiversity*, podcast, Spotify, 2025, https://open.spotify.com/artist/6lA7cVqwPG8jnz2dXBaWug.

4 Motiversity, podcast, YouTube, https://www.youtube.com/@motiversity.

Listen on Spotify[5] or at www.LewishHowes.com/sogpodcast.[6]

Find Everyday "Aha" Moments: *The Mel Robbins Podcast*

Mel Robbins offers relatable, inspiring, and actionable advice for building confidence and momentum. I always have "aha" moments when listening to her show.

Listen on Spotify,[7] YouTube,[8] and other streaming platforms by searching "Mel Robbins" or at www.MelRobbins.com/podcast.[9]

Master Your Mindset: *Tony Robbins*

Hearing Tony Robbins' mix of simple, powerful principles and clear explanations was the first time self-development truly landed for me. I started my career listening to his *Personal Power* cassette tapes and even walked across coals at one of his live events. His books and talks continue to inspire me today.

Find his events, books, and podcasts at www.TonyRobbins.com[10] or on YouTube.[11]

Get Inspired by Athlete Stories: *Autumn Athletes with Larry Sorenson*

---

5 Lewis Howes, host, *The School of Greatness*, podcast, https://open.spotify.com/show/07GQhOZboEZOE1ysnFLipT.

6 Lewis Howes, host, *The School of Greatness Podcast*, Greatness Media, 2025, https://lewishowes.com/sogpodcast/.

7 Mel Robbins, host, *The Mel Robbins Podcast*, podcast, Spotify, 2025, https://open.spotify.com/show/7vz4RYsD5MulTCrcH478t1.

8 Mel Robbins, YouTube, 2025, https://www.youtube.com/@melrobbins.

9 Mel Robbins, host, podcast, Mel Robbins, 2025, https://www.melrobbins.com/podcast/.

10 Tony Robbins, 2025, https://www.tonyrobbins.com/.

11 Tony Robbins, YouTube, 2025, https://www.youtube.com/@TonyRobbinsLive.

On his podcast, *Autumn Athletes*, Larry Sorensen interviews people who are "beyond their physical prime due to age or other life-changing events," yet they're still showing up to pursue big goals. Our conversation on his show gave me the chance to reflect on my own journey with physical fitness, mental toughness, and personal growth.

Listen on YouTube[12] or at AutumnAthletesNDY.com/interviews/.[13]

Peek Behind the Scenes of My World Record Attempt

This seven-minute video gives you a glimpse into my journey of attempting to break the world record for the longest female elbow plank. It captures the mental toughness, physical discomfort, and community support that went into my journey.

https://youtu.be/s9O72v-sbL8

Get Personalized Support: *Rise + Begin Wellness Coaching*

If this book sparked something in you, I offer wellness coaching to help you strengthen your mindset, embrace challenges, and move toward your own big goals. Work one-on-one with me to get the personalized tools, structure, and support you need to make meaningful changes in your life.

Visit www.riseshineco.com/coaching[14] for details.

---

12 Autumn Athletes… Not Done Yet, YouTube, 2025, Host: Larry Sorenson, https://www.youtube.com/@autumnathletesndy.

13 Larry Sorenson, Autumn Athletes… Not Done Yet, 2025, https://autumnathletesndy.com/.

14 Rashelle Mason, Rise + Begin, 2025, https://riseshineco.com/coaching.

ABOUT THE AUTHOR

Rashelle Mason is a wellness coach and the founder of Rise + Begin, a fitness instructor for the Princeton Club, and a loan officer at Waukesha State Bank. Drawing on her background as a nurse, executive leader, and lifelong athlete, she helps clients push beyond their comfort zones, feel more alive, and uncover new possibilities for personal growth.

Certified through NASM in wellness coaching, behavior change, nutrition, weight-loss therapy, and mindful drinking, Rashelle blends compassion, mindset work, and accountability to help clients create lasting change. Her approach is grounded in the belief that transformation begins the moment you decide to *just start*.

Through her attempt to break the world record for longest female elbow plank, Rashelle planked for five hours straight *eight* times and inspired hundreds along the way. She also rallied her community to raise over $20,000 for the Catch A Lift Fund, a nonprofit helping veterans find purpose through fitness. When she's not coaching or training, Rashelle loves spending time on the lake with her husband, Shan, teaching backyard yoga, and hiking with her kids, Tyler, Kyle, and Kole.

Rashelle offers wellness coaching and speaking events focused on mindset, motivation, and personal growth. To learn more or schedule a free thirty-minute virtual consultation, visit www.riseshineco.com.